TEN OF OUR TIME

Christians in Action

JOAN CLIFFORD

DENHOLM HOUSE PRESS
NUTFIELD · REDHILL · SURREY

First published 1967   © *1967 Joan Clifford*

SBN: 8521 3002 3

Printed in Great Britain by
Cox & Wyman Ltd., London, Fakenham and Reading

For
WYNNE HODSMAN
devoted servant of youth

THE AUTHOR wishes to thank all whose co-operation made this book possible; she is particularly grateful to those 'subjects' who found time in the midst of busy and exacting lives to talk to her about themselves and their beliefs.

CONTENTS

CONTENTS

EDITOR'S FOREWORD

This book tells of ten people. Assemble them in a group and anyone would be hard put to it to recognize any link between them. Yet they have something important in common. Each of them is a committed Christian, alive in the 1960's.

But they remain distinct and very different individuals. The expression of their faith follows no single pattern. It could scarcely in fact be more varied. This is part of the interest of their stories. One faith, but so many ways in which it works out in different people.

When Toscanini on one occasion had finished the rehearsal of a Beethoven symphony, the orchestra was so moved that they rose to their feet and applauded him. He hurriedly motioned them to be seated and in shocked tones said, 'Gentlemen, gentlemen; it is not I, it is Beethoven.' Paul the apostle would have understood that. 'I live, yet not I, but Christ lives in me.' This is Christian humility, as far removed as can be from false modesty. These ten people possess it, and on those terms alone have they consented to be included in this book.

'Are all the good Christians *dead*?' a youth is said to have complained. Much of the material available to teachers for illustration purposes makes his query understandable. So often it describes the life and work of people who, while worthy enough, have long since died. This book will help to reassure all who have felt the same misgiving. For here are Ten of Our Time.

A Pop Star's Faith

CLIFF RICHARD

The place is a small but comfortable dressing-room at that famous theatre, the London Palladium. Vivid modern pictures hang on the walls, there is a suave red telephone, and a large television set. A young man gets up to greet you; he is slim and dark-eyed, with a cap of smooth black hair, and a skin burned brown by the Indian sun of his early years, during the time when his father worked overseas. His manner is confident but courteous. His features are familiar; it is probably true to say that most people, from the youngest to the oldest and most 'square', would recognize 'pop' singer Cliff Richard, 'Golden Boy' of the contemporary scene.

Soon he will be out on the vast stage, delighting his audience, exercising his considerable artistry and, through his singing and relaxed, friendly personality, giving much pleasure to the hundreds of people in the auditorium. And afterwards there will be the familiar admirers at the stage-door, anxious to get a further glimpse of him and to have his autograph if they can get it.

Not so many years ago, Cliff wrote his own teen-age story, describing his happy childhood in Lucknow, Cawnpore and Calcutta. Among those naturally hazy memories, he recalled the exhilaration of a small boy flying the beautifully-made single sail kites, an important Indian pastime, with its own local champions, in which he joined. He told of his return home to England with his family and of the ensuing years of his boyhood here in an ordinary, normal, but close-knit family circle. His strong ties with his parents and his three sisters were self-evident, and the death of his father, after this book had been written, was obviously a great blow to him.

He revealed his intense feeling, in his early teens, for the 'beat' music of his own age, and his admiration for the current 'beat' idols. These, it seems, overshadowed a quite genuine hero-worship of footballer Stanley Matthews, and a satisfying skill in javelin-throwing. There was his important discovery that he himself had a voice, and could sing.

He spoke of the amateur group he formed whilst still at school, and the good times they enjoyed together; then the period when he worked as an office clerk, and formed in his spare time the 'Drifters', afterwards re-named the 'Shadows', the famous Group to which he is continually loyal and appreciative.

Looking back – a long way even from that pinnacle of nine-teen years – he retraced in his book the difficulties, disappointments and encouragements of those early days. There were neighbours to be placated, when fanatically-professional standards of playing were being striven after – living next door to a budding 'pop' group can be none too restful! There were parents to convince, and inner confidence to be attained for oneself. There was the first important booking, the first disc to be made, the excitement of building a vital personality and a genuine artist into the new name he had adopted, in place of the one given to him at birth – and there was the first exciting film.

He paid a sincere and heartfelt tribute to all the different people who had helped him on the way up, and he disclosed both the thrills and the snags of the climb to the top. Vividly he described the days 'before and after' the significant date in August 1958, when he made up his mind to turn professional. Schooldays were behind him, and so was his brief and unevent-ful commercial career. From that moment he entered the unique, killingly-competitive world of show-business, where everything is so much larger than ordinary life, and where it is tough even at the top.

It is now almost ten years since that day, and more has happened to Cliff than occurs to most people in the span of a whole lifetime. Fame and fortune became his; for seven years he was voted the most popular male singer in Britain. His popularity endures, and he has seen places and met people, achieved a position at the zenith of show-business and been presented to royalty.

'It's great to be young!' he cried as his teens drew to a close, but in the years that followed, life has obviously proved even more enthralling. Not everyone realizes, though, the relentless pace of life at the top, the endless travelling, the lack of personal privacy and inability to move just when and where you want, because of the insatiable curiosity of the public. These are the disadvantages of fame. There are the personality conflicts seemingly inevitable in the highly-charged atmosphere of the theatrical world, and the frustrations of alleged misrepresentation and misunderstanding, from both Press and public. How difficult, he seems to say, to make sure that people really understand what you did say and what you actually meant, and why it is so!

In spite of everything, however, it has been almost a decade of complete triumph, from a material viewpoint. The gold and silver discs, the contracts that ensure the good future, these have been symbols of happy days that need not end. And the people who have listened to the young singer have received cheerful and pleasant entertainment that appeals to all ages.

During the last few years, other ideas have been buzzing in the heart and mind of Cliff Richard. He has been led to the conclusion that his present mode of life may not satisfy him for the remainder of his working days. And this decision has come, not lightly, but as the result of a great deal of thinking and searching, and the challenge of enlightened friends. Here again he has experienced the cynicism and misunderstanding of some members of the public. The gibe that he has 'gone religious' is something he has had to take, along with the oft-repeated statements that his open assertion of his newly-accepted Christian faith is just a publicity stunt.

Certainly the old advice to declare your beliefs and let people know, has not been without cost to this young man. He broods upon the strange reactions of folk who simply cannot grasp that there is no 'angle' to his new position, except that of getting over loud and clear his determined adherence to the Christian faith.

Even now, he does not for a moment support the idea that it is impossible to carry on in show-business and still witness to his new-found faith. He is scornful of such an attitude and insists that show-business is 'just a job', like any other, and that as a practising Christian he can and must work out his faith from day to day in his daily occupation. He enlarged on this theme in a series of 'Five to Ten' radio programmes, and evidently feels this quite strongly.

Yet it is now generally known that he has said he means, during the next few years, to retire from his present way of life and teach Religious Instruction in school. This intention has been public news for quite some time and people at first wondered if the statement was a genuine one, and more than a well-meant wish. In his dressing-room, he states quite decisively that he does hope to leave show-business and train as a teacher.

'It is no rumour!' he says emphatically, and certainly seems determined. There are of course contracts to be worked out, and it is not exactly easy to terminate such a colourful and momentous career, in which many other people are bound to be involved for their livelihood.

'I shan't miss fame!' he declares, and is also positive that the gulf-like drop in income to be faced will not deter him. The question of his wealth, and its relation to his faith, has obviously caused him some heart-searchings, perhaps because the subject is frequently raised by questioners. 'I am not anywhere near to being a millionaire,' he smiles, but admits to many thoughtful conversations with clergy and with friends on the possible stumbling-block of his undeniable riches. He is well aware of the biblical warnings against the love of money. He says he concludes that the possession of money is not in itself a sin, but can see clearly that covetousness is indefensible. He again insists that, though he enjoys the fruits of his success, he does not count them as all-absorbing in life. There is so much more.

How and when did he become aware of this new dimension to life? How did he come to accept the Christian faith, that obviously now means so much to him? Questioned, he thinks it has been a gradual process, but that he has never needed to make the tremendous leap necessary for some people.

'My people were not atheists,' he says, 'there was always a Bible in our house, and a belief in God.'

Religion, meaning to him the Christian faith, underlay the life of his family, but possessed no very great or challenging personal meaning for him until about four years ago.

'I really began to read my Bible then,' he says, and it is evident that from this moment he was constantly looking for a fresh meaning to life and a clue to this in the Christian faith.

Help came from unexpected quarters. Rather typically, in the case of Cliff, who is at home with all age-groups, light was thrown on his searchings by an older person and also by some of his own contemporaries. In his youthful autobiography, he paid a sincere tribute to his English teacher at his former school, of whom he still speaks with admiration and affection. Here was a woman who plainly understood the potentialities of her pupil, and who had helped him through his O-level English examination in a subject he tackled well. More than this, she seems to have perceived in him some depths of personality not yet plumbed. Certainly in his own words, both written and spoken, Cliff attributes to Mrs. Norris, 'a real character' as he described her, a straightforward and helpful attitude that has benefited him on more than one occasion.

Mrs. Norris introduced Cliff to several young schoolteachers, who ran 'Crusader' groups and were keen evangelical Christians. Here were the contacts he needed. Now, within his own age-group, with people lively and well-informed at that, he could get to the root of things. In this congenial company, the dialogue went on.

Not only on church premises, but in ordinary social gatherings, the talk was animated, questions poured out.

'We talked about every subject under the sun, like all other young people do – religion, politics, sex – everything,' Cliff told a reporter. At casual meetings or at gay, cheerful parties, amid the clatter and the music and the small-talk, the stimulating conversations about life went on. And all the time, the young pop singer was searching, thinking, gradually meeting and facing the challenge of the Christian faith that was the background of the happy, fruitful lives of his new friends. He speaks particularly gratefully of the contribution made by two such friends, Bill and Graham, who were able to clear up for him many points that had hitherto puzzled him.

The searching continued, and Christians of many denominations added their testimonies and helped him on the pilgrim way. Then came the moment when it was clearly put to him by a young friend that it was 'time he made a decision'. He thought this over and decided this was true, and that he did intend to make such a decision; he felt he was able to do so now, and made plans to discipline his life accordingly. Attendance at church, so far as was possible in his hectic time-schedule, regular Bible-reading, and prayer-time, these must become part of his life from now on.

Above all, there was a personal committal to Jesus Christ which, he emphasizes, he feels is the most important thing of all. He is often surprised, he says, that this seems so often 'missing', so far as he can see, in the religious experience of people, and in their Christian education.

His Christian faith is not only a Sunday thing to him, nor solely a matter of religious disciplines; he sees clearly that it must work out in matters of everyday behaviour. As he has frequently told reporters, he may just not be the kind of person who naturally goes for living it up at night-clubs, or drinking heavily. But he does think that Christians should live by a considered moral code. He does think that sex outside marriage is plain wrong, and says he does not believe in divorce, or the re-marriage of divorced persons. Perhaps this high doctrine of marriage in these days has made him especially thoughtful about the question of his own marriage, which has not yet taken place; he obviously feels he must be quite sure when the time comes.

No doubt the happy home life he knew in his early days, with devoted parents, and the cut and thrust of brother-sister relationships, gave him a sturdy, healthy background, where unselfishness was recognized as a good thing, and there were loyalties beyond oneself. In the richer and even more promising life he has now embarked on, there are even more challenges, but infinitely greater thrills.

'You might say that was another great turning-point for me,' he confesses, speaking of one confrontation of an enormous audience that definitely had his nerves stretched. On this occasion, it was not a question of being out front to entertain, or amuse; it was not a matter of projecting one's personality to make the fans happy. He was there, in the vast arena at Earl's Court, London, to use his golden voice in the service of God in a particular way. At the request of Dr. Billy Graham, the American evangelist, he sang the gospel-songs which were so much more than entertainment; they were, in fact, his testimony to his faith, and his willingness to use his gifts in the highest possible way. He speaks of his nervousness at this time and his knowledge that his action would very likely be misunderstood by some. This turned out to be so; there were those cynics who, once again would attribute any action of this kind to the publicists. However, he is learning to come to terms with the strange habit of some people of denigrating the very idols they have set up, and is very sensibly deciding to try to ignore them. 'A great moment,' for him, Earl's Court, and he was very conscious of the huge audience, particularly of the crowds of young people present.

Asked if he feels a responsibility towards his own tremendous youthful following, he nods vigorously, and answers an emphatic 'yes'. He finds it difficult to understand the attitudes of some of his contemporary artists who disclaim any such responsibility. He knows that his words and actions are very much in the public eye and undoubtedly influence the youngsters who follow his career with such avid interest; he cares that he should give to them as good a lead as is possible.

The encouragement and admiration and friendship of young people has meant a lot to him, especially over the past few years. He himself tries to do what he can for the younger generation, by taking part in the leadership of the Crusader group in North London where he attends church, and by giving his services at special youth club functions and other similar events. In the future, he hopes, he will do even more, when he tackles the transition from pop star to R.I. teacher. He recognizes that he is no intellectual, but feels that, with enough concentration and determination, he can attain adequate standards, and this he intends to do; in fact, the studying at home has already begun. There will certainly be some problems for him, and the sinking of a public personality that has known the full limelight-treatment for many years. One may think it will also be none too easy for those whose task it will be to train him and accept him as just another ordinary student teacher!

However, Cliff is a very determined young man, and with the sustaining power of his newly-discovered Christian faith, it seems more than likely that he will succeed. He is certainly a fellow who knows his own mind and is not afraid to speak it. Very firmly he acknowledges his debt to the young Jehovah's Witnesses who helped him during his searchings. 'You can't help admiring their feeling for the Bible,' he says. Very plainly he talks of his own absolute belief in the need for a personal commitment to the Lord Jesus Christ.

Very definite too is his appreciation of the fine values to be found in so many of his young contemporaries, and his belief that there is nothing to prevent them too from finding the best kind of life in accepting the Christian faith.

'Somehow,' he says, 'you've got to get down to their level, and talk to them in their own language; they can surely be persuaded that it is the in-thing to be a Christian.'

Among those who can persuade them, there can be few more attractive advocates than this very twentieth-century young man, pop singer Cliff Richard.

2

'Do you want to argue?'

LORD SOPER

Not far from the grey walls of the Tower of London, that grim fortress so closely associated with the events of British history, an exceptional Englishman demonstrates weekly the national right of free speech and public assembly. A crowd gathers to hear him and between him and this audience, many of them 'regulars', ripples the ebb and flow of argument, with much vigour, plain-speaking and tough humour. The heckling has its own language and pattern, often fairly predictable, but there is plenty of razor-sharp sense among these exchanges, and an unerring return by the speaker to Christianity as the sole basis of world hope. Intellectually equal to all their questionings, yet with the common touch they can appreciate, he rides the waves of controversy with a skill and stamina born of long experience.

This familiar figure, uncluttered in appearance with his plain black cassock and smooth hair, now with hands on hips, now breaking animatedly into lively gesture, is the Baron Soper of Kingsway, Parson Extraordinary. He has offered Christ to the general public, each Wednesday in the open air on Tower Hill, for more than forty years.

Donald O. Soper, Methodist minister and Life Peer, is a man delighted to argue for the Gospel's sake. In one way or another, he has spent a lifetime proclaiming the Christian faith and advocating its supremacy. He is firmly of the opinion that the Good News should be presented in a satisfactory intellectual framework; the word 'THINK' – slightly suspect in some quarters – is high on his list of life-priorities, for both preachers and seekers. In his own particular idiom, he has practised his brand of theological and political wrestling throughout the many years of his ministry. On Tower Hill, in the House of Lords, in London's County Hall, on platforms and in the open air all over the world, on radio and television, the familiar, gravelly-baritone has been heard, putting forth the Soper views, often held to be disturbing. He has rigorously subjected the ideas of others to disquieting scrutiny. His opinions and beliefs have also been vigorously propagated in print, in books and articles.

Not unnaturally, so positive a personality could expect to meet opposition – even antagonism – and this has come about. A certain amount of criticism is no doubt stimulating, but reactions have often proved fierce to the point of bitterness. This is perhaps inevitable in the case of one treading so boldly on sensitive national, international and denominational corns. 'Pacifism and Socialism did not receive a friendly hearing in South Africa', as one friend reported; opinions on the royal observance of Sunday prompted a Mayoral Welcome cancellation; a stated willingness to endure world Communism rather than see a third world war raised a hornet's nest; pessimistic – or realistic – remarks concerning his own denomination's future caused a furore. He has concerned himself actively in issues such as the abolition of the death penalty and, more recently, supported the parliamentary reform of the laws concerning abortion, homosexual behaviour and gambling.

In some instances, antagonisms have been markedly personal and unpleasant; in one Commonwealth country he was snubbed by its Prime Minister; during World War II he was banned from the BBC; on a visit to Northern Ireland he received a stormy reception and had a Bible flung at him; he has been manhandled and knocked from his platform in Hyde Park; he is the constant recipient of unreasoning and abusive letters.

Yet, despite such apparent marks of disfavour and a far from unanimous appreciation of his activities, considerable honours have been given to him, far outweighing criticism. Among these he counts the Presidency of the Methodist Conference, and the Life Peerage conferred in 1965. For many people who cannot easily accept without qualification all his viewpoints, he still rates high as a parson genuinely and deeply concerned about world issues; for those who find themselves in total agreement with him, who have perhaps experienced the quickening of his leadership, he is a hero-figure of almost more than life-size. In any event, it is difficult to ignore or dismiss him and he is undoubtedly one of the most familiar clerics known by sight and sound to the man-in-the-street.

It seems that, even as a boy, the young Donald Soper had already decided that he wanted to be a minister. It no doubt seemed natural enough, in the traditional keen Methodist family setting in which he grew up, where the minister was respected and his vocation held high. Donald's father was the superintendent of the local Sunday school and a firm temperance advocate. This influence rubbed off on to his son, who signed the temperance pledge at the age of eleven and has not broken it yet. As he still says . . . 'it isn't that I regard drink as the devil in solution, or think one drink would pickle my intestines – it's just that the Kingdom of God is not sufficiently advanced for us to be complacent about the social menace of drunkenness . . . most of us have enough difficulty in steering straight when we are sober!'

Youthful days were happy ones; a brother and sister completed the talented and spirited family circle. A certain measure of Methodist discipline was imposed, but does not appear to have caused any resentment. When the family went on holiday each summer, to a seaside resort, the first resolute action after the Saturday arrival was the search for the local Wesleyan church, which would be attended next day. Only after this had been located was it permissible to rush off to the beach and abandon oneself to the holiday spirit.

The whole family was musically gifted. As children, the young Sopers usually received some small instrument in the annual Christmas stocking and were expected to produce a tune of sorts by breakfast-time. No doubt this initiation paved the way for the near-legendary recitals of merit given by Lord Soper upon the tin whistle at certain public meetings each year! Music has always meant much to him – he is an accomplished pianist and singer – and he has always ensured that

high musical standards have characterized the worship of the
churches within his care.

Schooldays seem to have presented few problems; when he
left to go up to Cambridge in 1921, he was captain of his school
and had demonstrated a general excellence in all spheres. A
report of later days from his former headmaster paid tribute to
the 'quite exceptional fellow', with his literary and musical
ability, sportsmanship far above the average and powers of
organization. The report also commented on 'D. O. Soper's
power of influencing those under him', this quality being a
'vast influence for good'.

University life for the young undergraduate was a confirming
yet liberating experience. Senior schooldays had been spent in
the shadow of the First World War, which naturally restricted
the movements and influences of those formative years. At
Cambridge, in a wider and more bracing intellectual setting, at
a time of considerable political and social ferment, there crys-
tallized some at least of the views on which henceforth his life
would be based. He became aware that there was a wider
world than the academic, wider too than the somewhat
proscribed Methodist circle in which he had previously made
his personal judgements. He was not yet ready to declare himself a convinced pacifist; on leaving school he had held the
position of R.S.M. in the school cadet corps and it was some
time before he made a radical decision here. Nor did he, during
these questing days, discover for himself the sacramental path
in his religious life that was to mean so much to him in later
years.

Yet Cambridge saw the awakening of his political consciousness, as well as the inner acknowledgement of the necessity for
evangelism that was never to be absent from his future
Ministry. He recalls a visit during those days to the railway
workshops at Derby, which greatly impressed him. He had
never really seen industry in action before this and was de-
pressed at the workers' conditions and his own conclusion that
this was what the capitalist system meant. Merely the tip of
the iceberg as it was, this visit set him to hard thinking; it
sealed for him the conviction that changes in working condi-

tions and happier lives for working people could come about only through political action; the Christian faith had to be politically expressed and, as far as he could see, this meant Socialism. Consequently, he joined the Labour movement and began forty years of close association with the Party.

Neither the greatly increased circle of his acquaintances at Cambridge, with their varying and challenging personal philosophies, nor the cynicism of post-war Britain in the early twenties, undermined his religious faith or his wish to become a parson. He subsequently offered himself as a candidate for the Methodist ministry, in the Church in which he had been brought up and to which he has always remained loyal, despite the intermittent disenchantments which he has voiced from time to time. Accepted by the appropriate committees and subjected to the considerable training programme of his denomination, he emerged at last to fill his first clerical station at Oakley Place, a church in London's Old Kent Road.

There could have been few more disturbing appointments. Conversation in the drab tenement streets here was a far cry from the intellectual cut-and-thrust of Cambridge, apparently remote from the thoughtful idealism of theological college. Here it was evident that the world 'fit for heroes' had plainly not arrived, and among this underprivileged community, 'pie in the sky' would never have appeared less welcome. Nor did the masses, men in particular, surge into church to hear his views on the way in which Christianity and politics entwined could bring them new hope. While the caring and worshipping ministry of the local church must go on, a platform had to be found for reaching these 'outsiders', for whom the Gospel was so wonderfully relevant. Choosing a site likely to prove fruitful for gathering an audience, the preacher set up his stand on Tower Hill. Here, following the example of his illustrious predecessor – John Wesley – he came to steely grips with the incredulity, cynicism, hostility, good-heartedness and sheer desperation of the ordinary working people. Gradually, his audience grew.

It was on this anvil that his pacifist philosophy was forged.

Arguing with his new friends in this free-for-all forum, he was finally convinced within himself that this was what the way of Jesus really meant. He became committed to this viewpoint, from which he has never since deviated. Characteristic of the new life of the Christian, he says, is what he now thinks of as 'non-violent love', a positive rather than a negative attitude. 'We must find an alternative to force,' he emphasizes, agreeing willingly that this is supremely difficult. But he remains firmly of the opinion that this is the only valid distinctive feature of our faith which finally lifts it above other religions. All this began as he hammered out the meaning of Christianity for modern times with his fellows on Tower Hill.

His apprenticeship served, he went on to a further ministry at Islington, now accompanied by his young wife, formerly Miss Marie Dean, whom he had married in 1929. At the Central Hall, work was carried out against the same harsh background of industrial depression, with its repercussions of unemployment and gradual loss of dignity for the idle men. The Soper convictions on religion and politics seemed to him more relevant than ever. The men who drifted into the church premises, to while away the pointless hours, were encouraged to take up simple crafts to pass the time and keep them from brooding too much. The minister looked around for all con- temporary means of communication which might touch the hearts and minds of the neighbourhood. He began a long acquaintance with Wardour Street and introduced film-shows which were well attended. Meanwhile, he continued to throw himself into his open-air work on Tower Hill, now established as a regular focus of confrontation.

In 1936, there was a final move to the West London Mission, henceforth to be a Soper platform, as well as a worshipping church and a centre of devoted and efficient social service. The aura of the former superintendent, the formidable Hugh Price Hughes, was still to be felt; indeed, Mrs. Hugh Price Hughes was still alive and very much head of the Mission Sisterhood. Gradually, in his own manner, the new superintendent took into his hands the manifold threads of Mission enterprise, and added some more of his own. Living conditions today are somewhat different, but Kingsway Hall still stands as an extremely vigorous social agency; a glance at the letter-heading reminds one of the very varied service offered by the numerous hostels under its control, giving loving care, and often hope, to the victims and misfits of our society, as well as to ordinary citizens in particular need. The administration of such a centre would indeed require the qualities of 'good organization' so early noticeable in the Soper make-up, though the superintendent himself would be the first to pay tribute to the lay and professional assistance he receives in this sphere. Certainly the all-round witness of the West London Mission is a patent example of the outward-looking church, very much involved with the lives and needs of the community.

Yet, at the same time, the central core – worship – has been maintained at Kingsway, with an increasing eucharistic emphasis. The celebration of the Sacrament of the Lord's Supper has grown continually more important to Donald Soper. He agrees that this probably began as a reaction from the somewhat austere services of his early Methodist association, and the lack for him of sufficient beauty and dignity in such forms of worship. More than this, he sees attendance at Holy Communion as his own 'royal road' to Christian experience, containing within itself all the elements of the Gospel, and he looks hopefully to a reunited Christendom, brought together at the Lord's Table.

A pattern of existence has been built by him which has gathered impetus during his thirty years of superintendency at Kingsway. Between his habitual office as a Methodist minister and the administration peculiar to the Mission's structure, he has interwoven his own distinctive and varied programme – or had it interwoven for him. Special honours and duties were laid upon him in 1953, as President of the Methodist Conference, and in 1965, on his elevation to 'another place'. The year 1966, for example, included such diverse activities as David Frost's celebrated 'Breakfast'; seconding the Humble Address to the Queen's Speech in the House of Lords; conducting service in the Crypt of the House of Commons; revealing his musical tastes (which proved to be catholic) in the radio programme 'Desert Island Discs', and travelling as a group-leader to Greece where, with scriptural nicety, he preached on Mars Hill.

Travelling has, indeed, taken him pretty well all over the world, mostly by invitation of the indigenous Churches and Universities, or on Peace Missions. These visits have included Japan, Russia, Poland, East Germany, Nigeria and Zambia, as well as the Commonwealth countries and the United States. Travelling on a less arduous scale is also a frequent 'tail-end-of-the-week' undertaking and he is often to be found speaking 'somewhere in England' on Thursdays and Fridays. Nothing, though, is allowed to interfere with his appointment with the people of Tower Hill each Wednesday, or the similar gathering at Speakers' Corner in Hyde Park on Sunday afternoons which he later instituted.

Time is a priceless commodity, even for so competent a self-organizer. Yet ordinary people in conversation with him do not experience that sense of being suffered rather than encountered that sometimes – understandably – characterizes audience with great men. Probably gregarious by nature, Donald Soper seems to enjoy the company of his fellow creatures and there is no lack of testimony to his gaiety, wit and genuine zest for social intercourse. It is perhaps this trait that so often wins over people who might otherwise find him quite resistable. One must regard as utterly human a cleric seen, during an interval between official commitments, happily munching peanuts and offering them around. On the other hand, respect must be paid to an all-powerful concentration that can palpably contain the entire situation of a great conference whilst, at the same time, absorbing test cricket scores from a tiny transistor radio pressed to the ear.

Perhaps it is constant movement that gives an impression of continuing youthfulness and energy; the habitual wearing of a cassock also conveys a certain timelessness, being apart from ephemeral fashion. Certainly it is hard to remember that the many positive Soper pronouncements are uttered out of forty years of clerical experience. He is well aware that he is a man of his own generation and that the young people of tomorrow's world have to make their own response to the ageless Gospel and their own interpretation of the Kingdom of God for them. Strategically placed as is Kingsway Hall in the British capital, with student-land not far off, he cannot but gain an acute impression of the vociferously-expressed spiritual, political and intellectual ferment of the young. They must make their own decisions and form their own priorities, with the question of World Peace almost certainly the terrible, urgent issue of the times.

As well as being the father of four daughters, with all the experience this has brought, he is in constant touch with youthful age-groups. It was his evangelical zeal that inspired and earlier sustained the Order of Christian Witness, which he still supports. For the Campaigns run by this organization, young people from all over the country are trained to formulate their beliefs and to witness to their faith in a variety of ways. In response to invitations from local churches, they engage in door-to-door visiting, open-air work, house groups. The explanatory leaflet, obtainable from Kingsway Hall, London, pulls no punches. 'Would you,' it asks, 'be prepared to spend a week of your holiday, pay for yourself and sleep rough in order to tell other people about Jesus Christ?' Each year between 150 and 200 members of the Order of Christian Witness do just that, and find tremendous satisfaction in the enterprise; they discover their own abilities in this form of service and make friendships often of lasting value. It is an exciting experience for the members, as well as for those to whom they go, and in initiating and encouraging this modern evangelism, Donald Soper has given the Church an up-to-date and burnished tool. In its three aspects, 'Communication', 'Community' and 'Communion', O.C.W. clearly reflects the emphases of its founder.

Fashions in thought change but, basically, Donald Soper sees no reason to cast aside the beliefs that have evolved during a lifetime. He still believes, in spite of some modern theological controversy, in the validity of the local church and the ordained ministry. The local church should be still 'right at the centre', he says firmly, reminding one of the long-standing Tuesday

Prayer Meeting at Kingsway, for so long a source of grace and renewal. The local church cannot simply be liquidated, but must remain as the sponsor and power-house of an effective out-going ministry.

Similarly, he is convinced of the continuing necessity for ordained ministers of the Church, a cadre of professionals. They might advantageously be trained in a more enlightened manner, with greater emphasis on the practical, but motivated in the traditional way by a genuine vocational impulse, and the desire for 'life service', tough yet satisfying.

He cannot but be aware of his own natural gifts and the likelihood that he would have made a distinctive mark elsewhere. The Law? Music? Drama? Full-time authorship? Professional politics? He seems to feel that the office of 'Minister of the Gospel' is the most fulfilling of them all; it seems a foregone conclusion that, if he 'had his time over again', he would ask for nothing more. His calling gives him an entrée into so many different spheres, the opportunity to influence people and win converts to the source of Christian power. And certainly nothing less than this power is needed to bring about the Kingdom of God as he conceives it. For to him it is a 'place in which all will have somewhere to live, enough to eat, and time to say their prayers, and where little children need not be afraid if they hear a bang in the night'.

No doubt he will go on arguing that this is truly so, to the end of the line. . . .

3

Office Boy to Boardroom . . .

S. M. TENNICK

London Airport coming up! . . . Fold those papers and stuff
into a brief-case . . . leave the mental calculations for the time
being . . . on the runway now . . . hurry down the steps . . .
through the customs . . . catch the train . . . home at last . . .
family running out to greet you . . . laughter and small gifts to
unwrap . . . roses out in the garden . . . everything the same . . .
peaceful really after those hectic days. . . .

Relaxing at length in a comfortable arm-chair, S. M. Tennick
reflected that business trips like this were always stimulating
but tiring too . . . pleasant . . . one privilege of the executive
life, but definitely hectic . . . all go, go, go. . . .

For a great number of such business men, thoughts like
these must have marked the conclusion of a visit to Canada on
the occasion of Expo 67. Who could fail to be invigorated by
the great Exhibition? How exciting were the cross-currents of
cosmopolitan activity, industrial challenge, and the visual
interest of the fantastic national pavilions! To say nothing of
the fabulous transatlantic hospitality. An experience to remember. And for many commercial visitors, the satisfaction of
returning home with full order books and sealed contracts.
And so it goes on . . . this year Canada, last time the States;
soon, maybe, the Continent . . . the world grows yearly smaller
and today's men of business have to girdle it to stay in the race.

One British industrial director lately back from Expo 67,
S. M. Tennick, born and bred on Teeside, is as fully aware as
anyone can be of the particular assets and problems of the
North-east. Unsentimental and unaffected, entirely devoid of
delusions of grandeur, 'S. M.' would certainly never think of
himself as a 'Captain of Industry'. There is no evidence that, as

a very young man, he brooded on the possibility of making a
million, or started up a one-man plant in his back yard. Indeed,
his youthful interests he sums up concisely in a few words –
'Mad keen on sport!'

Nevertheless, he is probably typical of many of his contemporaries – convinced of the need to make a success of his corner
of the industrial field, on both personal and national scores. To
this end, he knows that one must be thoroughly efficient.
Furthermore, in company with a probably lesser number of
colleagues, he does his best to carry out his business duties as a
professing Christian, his Nonconformist conscience providing
certain standards of behaviour with which he tries to comply
This can never be a simple matter and during the journey from
office boy to managing director, he has had to revise some of his
preconceived notions and do some considerable re-thinking.

All this, however – the hazard of joining society's 'Coronary
Belt' and the tension arising from Christian principles – would
have seemed a world away in the 1930s. Here was a teenager
almost fanatically absorbed in tennis, cricket and, above all, in
soccer – that magnetic distraction that dominates the north of
England. Ecstasy was in the air as he hurled himself about the
field; young Sid Tennick, with some brawn as well as brains,
revelled in the game and fancied little better. He was fiery too,
in those days . . . on one occasion a difference of opinion flared
up between himself and another player, a matter of deadly
earnest at the time. A third player – and friend – wishing to act
as peacemaker, hurriedly pinioned Sid's arms behind his back,
whereupon the opponent took a swipe at his protagonist and
knocked him out. 'Turning the other cheek' henceforth took on
a new meaning.

Companionship meant much to him in those days, many
friends belonging to the football and badminton teams of his
local Methodist church. His parents were glad for their son to
have some religious association; after the customary years in
Sunday school, he was 'held' in adolescence by the recreational
and sporting facilities wisely provided at the chapel. And, as
time went by, the general atmosphere engendered something
more than team-spirit. Almost unconsciously, 'chapel values'

began to permeate his life. Widening experiences in the years
to come would take him, for a time, far from the small though
quite noteworthy Teeside town of his boyhood, with its important railway yards and water coolers, and pleasant verging
countryside. Long years of war would stiffen the sinews of
character and provide invaluable knowledge of human nature;
more sophisticated contacts would impinge upon his life,
challenging the black and white standards and simple judgements of teenage years. Yet basic values, deeply assimilated,
would endure.

On leaving Grammar School, with no clear thoughts as to the
future, young Tennick entered a local manufacturing firm, a
private company, and was initiated into the mysteries of office-
boy status. Along with the tea-making and general duties, he
began to acquire some plain facts about the end-product of the
firm's existence and how the business really worked.

Like all young fellows, he came up against the predicament
of principles from time to time, and had to make his own ethical
judgements in awkward situations.

Sometimes, he would saunter, whistling, along the corridor
to the Board Room, summoned on some minor errand by the
peremptory telephone. As he shot in and out of the 'holy of
holies', he had no idea that, one day, he himself would sit at the
long, gleaming table, in one of the vast, shiny chairs from
which the 'old buffers', as he thought of them, ruled the firm's
affairs in majesty.

Time passed and he became assistant cashier; there were
now studies to be undertaken. Life was altogether more responsible these days, particularly since he had by now married
the attractive and vivacious brunette from the local Methodist
church who was to be his helpmeet in so gracious and stylish
a manner in the demanding years ahead.

Suddenly, it seemed, war clouds were gathering, then breaking dramatically in 1939. For the next six years, along with the
majority of his contemporaries, Sid had other and more urgent
matters to think about. His transition through the ranks, from
private to sergeant and later to commissioned officer, with
special training duties, gave him unique experience of authority

and its problems, and unequalled opportunity for learning the tactics of human relations. Sweating on the beach at St. Nazaire, haggling in Indian markets, licking very raw N.C.O.'s into shape on the North-West Frontier – he was seeing life in the rough, and testing many of the theories and values formerly taken for granted.

The bronzed and quietly mature young man in the unfamiliar civvy suit who returned to the office he had left – surely a century ago! – was now ready to shoulder heavier responsibilities; he was eager to make up for lost time, and to press ahead. He admitted to himself that he had changed somewhat. This was indeed to some extent even physically true; he had acquired, besides sunburn and a tough exterior, a slight deviation to his nose – the result of the surgeon's knife at the conclusion of a shipboard boxing-match; perhaps the young lieutenant had overestimated his capability in the ring. . . .

He discovered now that not only had he altered a little, but that things were different too in his old stamping-grounds. During his absence, his firm had joined with another neighbouring company and become a public company. He was appointed Office Manager of the enlarged outfit, and set himself to master the new situation.

In the strange and sometimes uncomfortable process of readjusting to civilian conditions, he found an ideal focus for reorientation. The men's movement known as the Regnal League, founded in his local church prior to 1939 by a farsighted person, had been held together during the straitened war years by a faithful few. When the battle veterans returned, some bore the marks of deep and understandable inner disturbance; it was not to be expected that the general brutality of war and the horrors of prison-camp experience could leave them untouched. Mercifully, 'Regnal' was still very much alive and kicking, and waiting to welcome and heal. Sharp were the verbal thrusts enlivening the free-for-all discussions that characterize this out-going and all-embracing organization. During the long and uninhibited sessions of argument, earthy humour, confession, sharing of experience and sheer hot air, the church's young men hammered out their personal philosophies and sought to reconcile these with the teaching of Christ as they were constantly hearing this expounded. The parson chipped in, but as a fellow-member, on an equal footing.

Sid was grateful for this lively fellowship, 'free from humbug', as he puts it and, as time passed, for the chance to serve Regnal, both locally and at higher levels. That his contribution, 'sound judgement and wise counsels', has been valued is evident from the willing testimony of 'Dai Sam', General Secretary of the League. Speaking of the 'deep insight and strength of purpose' behind the 'unassuming personality', Mr. Samuel is proud to claim the personal friendship of Sid Tennick, as he has come to know him over the years, and to pay tribute to a consistent loyalty to the Regnal movement.

The integrity that soon became evident to Regnalism was not unnoticed by the 'powers-that-be' in Sid's firm; promotion continued steadily, through the positions of Company Secretary and Commercial Director. As the years passed, 'S.M.' was forced to admit to himself the sheer impossibility of adopting in industry the rigidly black and white evaluations he had once thought essential. He had to accept and live with, in the first place, the competitive principle on which much of the world's business life is run and, looming large behind this, the acquisitive streak in human nature so relentlessly demanding instant satisfaction.

Also, he was brought face to face with the tremendous variation in materials, machines, approaches to capital, skills and personalities, employed in modern industry.

Within such a set-up, any human being who did not intend to be broken by useless scruples, had perforce to accept some compromises – the 'greys' which Sid feels have simply got to be agreed upon in modern industrial practice. This is certainly not to imply a ditching of principles but the acknowledgement of the impossibility of waving a magic wand and applying an instant solution to all problems. Instead of dreaming of Utopia, life has to be lived in existing conditions of conflict and tension; the best that most Christians can do is to try to bring balance into situations as they arise, by decisions which may sometimes appear to be 'grey'. An acceptance of this view-point, 'S.M.' feels, released him from the stultifying guilt complex which, as he puts it, still 'inhibits so many Christian warriors'.

Brought up sharply now against the problems of modern industry, more and more deeply involved, Sid was continually thankful for domestic happiness, and for the fellowship and opportunities of his church-life. An ever-open door has always characterized his home, exceedingly pleasant though never pretentious, and for over twenty years countless visitors have gathered round his hearth and found a warm but unaffected north-country welcome. The two daughters who joined the family circle have added their particular gaiety and charm to the scene and it is undoubtedly true to say that no more active example of the 'church that is in the house' could be found than within the walls of the Tennick home. People come and go, call and chat, talk deeply and seriously, laugh and relax, welcomed by a delightful and popular hostess and a host who, though undemonstrative by nature, has great good humour and appetite for living.

His local church placed more responsibility on Sid, claiming valuable time, as did also the Regnal League. He knew that he could hardly refuse such duties, for as time went by, he was conscious of a deep debt to the church and the League. 'Blessed with many parsons who could think', as he puts it, he believes that some of their thoughts rubbed off on to him, and challenged his own views. He found himself given opportunities of service involving the making of far-reaching decisions and undertaking important organization. It took time, certainly, but it was interesting and, sometimes, genuinely exciting, as when Christian colleagues could be stirred to a 'new look', and to some hitherto unthought-of enterprise.

Rushing in where angels might have hesitated, he campaigned at his local church for the establishment of a new Youth Club. Older officials of Sid's church demurred at first; perhaps some of them found it difficult to accept that he himself, known to them since boyhood, was no longer a youth, but a man of mature years and judgement. There were endless conferences and explanations; money would have to be spent, and hard-headed northerners, Christians notwithstanding, must be convinced that 'the brass' would be wisely spent. Ultimately agreement was given and plans laid; providentially, all went well and the Opening Night saw a swarm of lively, curious youngsters pushing through the doors. The tale of the Club at 'Eastbourne' is now an old story. Completely re-designed today, and served by a full-time Youth Leader sustained by appropriate local authority grants, it witnesses with distinction in the area, and is by no means unknown, effective-wise, in administrative circles.

In its early days, Sid Tennick gave the lead that counted and pulled the new baby firmly to its feet. He was helped and followed by a succession of strong leaders, mostly at first other men of the Regnal League. Perhaps his deepest and most natural pride would come from the growth of new young leaders within the club itself; there was a thrill in seeing an independent-minded, attractive young adult, one who had begun as a noisy teenager in the club's early days, now well set in the saddle and coping admirably.

In 1960, 'S.M.' found himself Managing Director of his company which, a few years later, was to be taken over to become part of a larger group of companies. His office door bore the new and significant title. He was now fully extended as a business man and very much aware of the pressures of the position; deeply involved in personnel relationships, he was once again reminded of the complexity of these, and of the differing backgrounds, educational, cultural, hereditary, of the people with whom he worked at various levels.

Speaking generally of human relations in industry, he says today that these are no different than in other spheres; the basic requirement of success here seems to be mutual respect. This, he still feels, cannot be achieved without both sides being true to their word – with perhaps a major responsibility upon management – and remembering that all are human beings. Perhaps when talking of one's 'word' it must be recognized that in the quickly changing scenes of industry today, this 'word' may need to be altered suddenly. When this happens, as for example, in a situation of sudden redundancy, explanations ought to be reasonable and to be made intelligible to those to whom they apply.

Apart from the present concern for the lower-paid worker, 'S.M.' feels today that, by and large, the most vicious contentions splitting management and unions are disappearing. Excessive sentimentality which, for fear of hurt or change, permits men to 'rot' in inactivity should, in his opinion, be ditched. These views have been forged over a period of years, the direct outcome of first-hand experience. Personnel problems, the relentless challenge of foreign competition, long hours and hard work, all have combined to stretch and test. Yet throughout it all, 'S.M.' has managed to retain a personal equilibrium and a reputation for fairmindedness and consistency. He is happy to concede that his Christian faith has helped him to maintain a good degree of poise in the midst of tension.

Sometimes he becomes indignant, not least at Christian attitudes towards modern industrialized life. His belief in the importance of a Gospel relevant to the social needs of today has led him to contribute to an interesting ecclesiastical experiment. The Teeside Industrial Mission is now ecumenical, comprising several full-time Church of England parsons and one Methodist. This vigorous team is trained to act as a catalyst in the industrial field, and an extension of the 'parish ministry' to the factory floor, through the co-operation of management.

The Mission has also sponsored groups of managers and some trade unionists (by no means all church members), who meet informally outside business premises to discuss mutual problems and gather information on their particular region. S. M. Tennick has for several years belonged to such a managers' group in his home-town. Unassertive by nature, he has yet consented to put forward the position and views of industrialists to clerics at high level, and to theological students at a Durham College. 'S.M.' can certainly talk to them from long experience and strong conviction. Whilst honouring the Christian witness in hospitals, prisons and the like, he is deeply concerned for a 'preventive' as well as 'curative' witness.

'Surely the areas of everyday living, including industry, are where the casualties occur?' he urges. . . .

With the passing of time, he has become rather more comfortable in figure; athletics and soccer have now given place to golf. Yet his approach to life is still youthful. As well as attending business conferences, or Regnal functions, advising at important church meetings, or entertaining foreign visitors for his firm, he can still be seen ferrying car-loads of young people between home and church, and welcoming them easily to his fireside.

That he is known informally by his personal friends as 'old man Tennick' is not an indication of the passing years, but rather of the affection in which this unassuming man is held, the recognition of warm-hearted consistency.

The same friends will agree cheerfully that Sid has his prejudices; one lists his 'pet hates' as 'artificiality, self-righteousness, and feminine traits in men'. An acknowledged weakness too is no secret. . . . a lack of skill with tools . . . in his hands these seem to behave like poltergeists, darting mischievously about and misbehaving. Both he and his wife have long accepted that no handyman need fear competition from this quarter!

However, 'S.M.' presses forward and upward – with both feet firmly on the ground. Failures there are bound to be for this Director of Industry for, as he would certainly tell you, he is 'only human'. . . .

4

In the Tolpuddle Line . . .

JOHN BOYD

There was a scuffle and some shouting; the boys twisted easily
away and ran off, outpacing without difficulty the stout copper
who chased half-heartedly after them. The police could hardly
bring themselves to act very harshly towards these young lads
who were hanging round the coal dump. A few lumps of coal to
take home to an empty grate, no doubt that was the quest, but
who could really blame them? In the bad times of the years in
the early thirties, standards were almost bound to fall, and who
could be surprised? Youths; strong, lively, who ought to have
been hard at work, knew idle, hopeless days. No jobs, food and
heating scarce, it was no wonder principles sometimes went by
the board. Smaller boys were affected too; who could be surprised that this scavenging went on?

Among the group was one who would never forget these
times, on whom the experiences of these hard days would put
an indelible stamp. This small lad would grow into a tall,
broad-shouldered, vigorous man, but all the same, his whole
attitude and the direction of his life was to be largely governed
by them. Not to be forgotten was the ensuing humiliation of a
year of so-called 'unemployment', when he actually worked
tirelessly selling newspapers to augment the family income; not
to be entirely hidden away in the memory were the visits to the
soup-kitchens for a bowl of something warm and sustaining.
Motherwell, Scotland, in the early thirties – then mainly a
mining area – was not much of a land of promise for the young,
like many another place at that time.

Like other young people, John Boyd had had his dreams and
these did not include the pits, slag-heaps and steel furnaces of
his native heath. He wanted very much to be either a minister

or a doctor, both respected professions in Scotland, but in his heart he felt that such a future was very unlikely indeed. His parents were in no position to help such dreams to materialize, particularly during the fateful era when their son was growing to manhood. The five years at night-school that followed a secondary modern education – no 'day-release' study then – would help a determined young man towards the important tasks in front of him, but would not lead to either the pulpit or the consulting-room. Yet this early confrontation with the grim facts of life, a training in the 'University of Adversity', a phrase trite but true, was invaluable. It is perhaps not for nothing that the iron and steel industry has played so large a part in his life; certainly he developed an iron disregard of obstacles, and a steely determination to make himself felt, on committees, councils, executives, in all the places where power lies, for the accomplishing of action. And getting action has involved him throughout his life.

John Boyd makes no bones about his belief in the necessity of power. 'Most men love power,' he asserts simply, 'and if you have it, you can get things done.' Yet he seems to sense very clearly the dangers and temptations of power, and is himself plainly anxious that it be always used well. He himself, during almost half a century of living, has assumed considerable authority in the fields of trade unionism and politics. As an Executive Councilman of the Amalgamated Engineering Union, and also as Chairman of the Labour Party, until the autumn of 1967, he moves in power-spheres, and is willing and able to accept responsibility. He also serves as Vice-Chairman of the National Joint Industrial Council for the United Kingdom Atomic Energy Authority, Secretary of the National Craftsmen's Co-ordinating Committee of the Iron and Steel Industry, and Secretary of the Craftsmen's National Negotiating Committee of the Papermaking and Boardmaking Industry.

One would be right in attributing considerable qualities to this vital man, efficiency being markedly among them. Seated squarely in his large, airy room at the headquarters of the A.E.U., a room indicative of order but also of buzzing activity, he cheerfully agrees that he is 'ruthlessly efficient'. He implies that this is essential in the Executive which controls such a huge outfit. Yet there is a warmth of personality about him that rules out any conception of robot-like authority. His approach to his subordinates seems affable; when talking in the pleasant Scottish accent he still retains, his manner is animated, and his eyes twinkle. He is accustomed to command, a 'bonny fighter', but his humanity is self-evident.

There is another side to his life, and it is probably this that helps to contain, direct and refine the positive characteristics that are so innate a part of his make-up; in his membership of the Salvation Army, opportunities are found for his vigour and assertiveness, and he accepts the disciplines of the Army as willingly as any other member. To the Army he gives the same whole-hearted allegiance that typifies all his involvements.

John was only nine years old when, attracted by the Boys' Band, he became interested in the Army. His parents, he says, were indifferent to religion, but did not prevent him from pursuing this new enthusiasm. There was for him a genuine sense of release and fulfilment in the bold, martial-music-making of the band, and he welcomed the comradeship of the other boys.

Gradually, the ideas and beliefs behind the Army's trappings took hold of him too, and the 'Code of Honour' of a Christian was explained to him. His spirit was kindled; he too would fight in the Crusade against evil, and experience for himself the peace and joy of the forgiven sinner, and know the love of God! At last, he signed the Articles of War and of Faith and was proclaimed a Salvationist. From thenceforth, his Christian belief was to be the bulwark of his life, and his participation in Army practices intermingled significantly with his workaday activities. As he went forward, his faith and his life grew to-gether, more strongly and surely as the years passed. For him, this in fact is the only way to live, though occasionally his un-compromising religious adherence can be costly for him.

After his unpromising plunge into adult life, he became apprenticed, in 1931, as an engineering apprentice with a steel firm, where he worked for six years, emerging as a fully time-served engineer. He was interested in his job, even more interested in the conditions of work of those who laboured in this vital industry. Burning with social zeal, he joined his union at once, and at the same time became a member of the Labour Party. He does not deny that a fairly tough upbringing inevitably conditioned his attitudes. At any rate, even at this early age, the overall pattern of his life's future interests was fairly set. The Salvation Army, the job, the Union, and the Party, was enough for any man, even one so full of vigour as John Boyd.

Later, another – and eminent – influence entered his life, in the person of his wife. Nowadays, with their two daughters, they constitute a formidable and effective combination, all members of the Songster Brigade of the Army, devoted and happy in a noticeably joyful domesticity. John pays an obviously sincere tribute to the companionship and support of the attractive, creative home-maker who has shared his life for so many years – a life that was surely an unpredictable proposition at the commencement of their partnership!

'Headlong into the sea of toil,' to quote words often chosen by John Boyd as typical of himself, plunged the young reformer. When only twenty-one, he began a stint of five fighting attempts to win an Opposition seat in the municipal elections of his home-town. Offered a 'safe seat', he characteristically spurned it; he did not gain the seat for which he battled, but he relished the fight!

Developing his talents within the Union, he was constantly learning; absorbing knowledge of men and affairs, learning how to assess situations, and gaining confidence as a speaker and negotiator. He became aware of powers of leadership within him, and of an ability to win a response from his own oratory and persuasion. It was not long before the occasion arose for him to put these powers to the test.

Thrown up as an automatic leader, he found himself leading the 1937 Clydeside apprentices' revolt. He was in the thick of the fight, the struggle for better conditions and monetary increases for the lads whose difficulties he knew so well. Somehow, the combination of steel and warmth prevailed. Even now, he remembers this event with satisfaction and quiet pride, mixed with a little rueful humour! As a result of his leadership, the apprentices benefited quite considerably from a monetary point of view. The apprentices, but not he himself! As he says, 'by the time the award was made, I had ceased to be an apprentice, and had become a craftsman!' . . .

Nevertheless, the victorious outcome of this engagement confirmed his belief that there was work, and valuable work, to be done within the Union. From these early days, until he was about thirty years old, he was continually in office as a shop-steward. It was only his sense of the need to keep a proportion in his activities, that stopped him from taking an even more active part in T.U. affairs at that time.

When he was twenty-nine, however, he was elected as the youngest member in the history of the Amalgamated Engineering Union as a full-time official. He is still very much a 'young man' in this sphere. In 1953 he became a member of the Executive Council of the A.E.U., where he still serves. From 1963 to 1964 he became President of the Confederation of Shipbuilding and Engineering Unions, the youngest man ever to hold this post.

Similarly, he made progress in the ranks of the Labour Party, where his capabilities were soon recognized, and has served for eleven years on the Labour Party National Executive.

'In politics, I have never joined cliques,' he says with a grin. 'I am often at loggerheads with widely differing factions!' He repeats this, and makes it clear that he is very much 'his own man'. Yet his devotion to his Party and its cause is also plain, and obviously recognized and accepted as shown by the high honours accorded him.

An apparently strong physique and an indomitable faith allow him to pursue, with energy and success, a busy life of service for the Salvation Army which he loves. Here, much of his concern, both earlier and also today, is with young people. From the age of eighteen, until he left Motherwell, he was Young People's Sergeant. Harking back to the past, he talks with tremendous enthusiasm of 'his' Sunday school which, under the Army's aegis, he built up 'from nothing', in an unemployed workers' hut in Motherwell when he was young.

Here, in a slum area, with an appeal as powerful as that of the Pied Piper, he drew in from one hundred and fifty to two hundred children, to hear the story of Jesus and His love. John worked here with unabated happiness until he left Motherwell to go and live in Paisley.

He was a club leader for five years, and Youth Secretary among the Salvation Army 'Torch-bearers' for five years; the membership, he recalls, never dropped below thirty. With obvious delight, he speaks of these adventures, as they seem truly to have been, when he has been able to imbue the youngsters in his charge with his own brand of infectious and gay enthusiasm.

The officer in charge of the Citadel to which he now belongs, paying a tribute to his versatile member, speaks of the 'fun and laughter' which John Boyd so often inspires.

'John is always in demand as a Master of Ceremonies,' says the Brigadier in question, 'and when he is in the chair, one can always be sure of an evening of real fun and games.'

No doubt his zest for living, and his gay, friendly spirit, endeared the young people to their leader throughout the whole of his service for youth, and have made it easy for him to proceed to deeper levels of direction at the appropriate moment.

Then, as now, he has been capable of this. 'A good time for all' is never the sole goal in his contacts with others. As a Recruiting Sergeant among Salvationists, he has a duty to counsel the religious seeker at the penitent form to a proper understanding of the Christian faith, and to lead him or her into a personal relationship with Jesus Christ that can be genuine and permanent. To kneel beside any such seeker, whether young or older, in the capacity of counsellor, must be a solemn undertaking, needing qualities even more intense than those required for the day-to-day life of the Union or the Party. Yet he is not afraid of his responsibilities here either; particularly is he glad when a young fellow or girl accepts the claims of Christ upon their lives.

Understanding young folk is very important to John. He knows clearly that both in the church and in the world, so far as these can be separated, consideration must be great for those who will make up the future generation. Asked about his views on the teenagers of today, and their slightly older brothers and sisters, he is in the main optimistic.

'I try to look beyond the extremes,' he says, 'and I feel there are as great reservoirs of good as ever there were. After all, the youth of today have much greater temptations and many more problems than before . . .'

He is also convinced that the youth of today present a far greater challenge to their seniors than hitherto. 'They challenge adults much more than my generation did when young,' he feels, indicating a respect for the frankness, questioning and lack of hypocrisy of youngsters now.

He has plenty of opportunity to ponder on their views and outlook. This is not only because of the two lively daughters who are, he implies, his most candid critics, and of whom he is justly proud. Cath and May are deeply involved in Salvationist life, like their parents; both have musical talents, and give of their varying gifts in prodigal fashion. John Boyd is in constant touch with the younger generation through his Army activities. More than this, he is also much concerned about the place of young people in the Union which he serves, and in the trade union world generally. Recognizing that the terrible, dynamic impulse of suffering that goaded his own generation to action no longer exists, he accepts that another basis for service is needed. This concerns him very much indeed and the question of how to attract youth into the unions is one that he is continually facing. Can the unions be better geared to draw the country's youth? In his own private thought, and in the Annual Youth Conferences, attended by young people from all over Britain, these matters are being thrashed out and kept very much to the fore. Asked if there are opportunities for today's youth in the trade unions of the present time, he nods emphatically. Youngsters cannot be all that different, he seems to reflect.

A 'whole-hogger' for the interest that dominate his life, John has little time for so-called 'hobbies'. He reads a good deal, and the books and documents that he must study are frequently absorbed during train journeys. Perhaps a bit of attention to a 'wee garden' may count as a hobby!

One could hardly expect a figure that seems rather larger-than-life to cram any more into his days. In everything he does the word 'Big' seems to come to mind . . . as a fighter for the faith, as a warrior for man's dignity and worth as a workman, as one who uses his voice to the Glory of God, he comes over Big! It does not seem surprising that, despite his gruelling time-schedule, he is 'always ready to speak in an open-air meeting', as his Salvationist officers testify. And as well as singing with the rest of his family in the Songster Brigade, he thoroughly enjoys playing that big instrument – the Double B-flat Bass – none larger in the local Band! Armed with this gleaming giant, he lifts heart and sound to praise his Maker.

It has been a long journey since the bold brass called him as a small boy into the Salvation Army's portals, though he is now only 'in his prime'. He has since filled with distinction positions both spiritual and temporal of great importance, and there may be others to follow. Testimonies to his abilities and character abound; he is obviously held in high esteem throughout the Army world, and the officer commanding his local corps at the Catford Citadel speaks of their 'privilege and honour to have him as a soldier there'.

Moving to wider fields, he has been called the 'ideal combination of Christian and Trade Unionist', though this very intermingling has brought him criticism in a few cases from political opponents. He is restrained in speaking of the past struggles in which his doughty character has been forged. Those who know him well feel justified in rating him highly among the world-fighters for decent working standards and values. Without hesitation, the Rev. 'Bill' Gowland of the Luton Industrial Mission talks of John Boyd as being 'in the direct succession of the Tolpuddle martyrs' . . . And one could not say much more than that.

5

The Road to Westminster ...

GEORGE THOMAS M.P.

There are some who still remember those days, when the young orator seemed to be on fire, metaphorically speaking! His musical Welsh tones rose and fell and there was passion and conviction in his utterances; reason too. With the utmost animation, he pressed home his point. There were murmurs of approval and people were swayed. Not everyone agreed with him, naturally, but all were exhilarated. George had the 'hwyl' again!

At the Men's Parliament, flourishing in the Tonypandy Methodist Mission during the years preceding the Second World War, no brighter star had risen than young Thomas. In the political debates he made sharp use of the teeth of eloquence cut originally in the Mission's Wesley Guild and in the Methodist pulpits where he was increasingly welcome. Somehow, when this slim figure began to speak, religious convictions and political awareness were inevitably intertwined.

The Parliament was no joke; procedural rules were strict and members delighted in the cut and thrust of debate. No holds barred, there was a vigour and reality about its activities that encouraged men to take it seriously. And it was a wonderful stamping-ground for budding talent. Matters discussed were very much more than hypothetical. During the black days of economic depression, the mining community of the Rhondda Valley suffered badly. The Methodists at Tonypandy recognized the absolute primacy of offering a ministry of practical compassion, where not only souls but bodies too received consideration. The Mission provided cheap meals, a toy-making centre and a boot repairs depot; through this enlightened caring, it declared the essential oneness of social concern and evangelism.

Among its members, young George Thomas, ardent Welshman and Methodist, was whole-hearted in his agreement with the Mission's avowed policy; perhaps unconsciously, he absorbed this conception of the Christian faith into his bloodstream. Certainly, belonging to the Tonypandy Mission was one of the important influences that led him from the novitiate of the Mission 'Men's Parliament' to the House of Commons, and propelled him along the road of destiny that was to take him from Wales to Westminster.

One of his ministers at the chapel, a 'Christian Socialist', as he describes him, made a keen impression on the enthusiastic debater. This had the result of drawing George, then still in his teens, into the political scene. Here he began to work out for himself the meaning of the practical application of the Gospel to the running of everyday affairs.

Further back still, a potent formative figure laid the foundations of his future achievements. A remarkable mother, steeped in Methodism and deeply interested also in politics, brought up the little boy who would later leave the valleys for much wider spheres. A devoted woman, shrewd too, she came of staunch stock. Her father, John Tilbury, described as a patriarchal character, was much involved in the erection of the Tonypandy Mission, and had been asked to perform the opening ceremony. Day by day, he had gone eagerly to watch the masonry mounting higher and higher. This proud task, alas, he was never able to carry out, since he died before the arrival of the great day. His unquenchable enthusiasm and reverence for the chapel were passed on to his daughter and she, in her turn, inspired her young son to similar attitudes.

George was born in Port Talbot, round about the beginning of this century, and before he could form any opinions about his birthplace, the family moved back to the Rhondda Valley, which came to mean so much to him. With typical Welsh fervour, he grew up deeply attached to his native land, though he does not go along even now with militant nationalism, as he makes very plain. The years of his teens were packed with interest, certainly for George himself, as he discovered his varying and considerable gifts.

There was the Youth Club which he ran in Tonypandy, where he needed to pit all his wits, and summon all resources, to make the grade with his lively young contemporaries.

'I guess teenagers were as difficult then to manage as they are supposed to be now,' he confesses with a smile.

In the youth drama group, he took on the job of producer, and found tremendous interest here. 'Like all true Welshmen, I loved the theatre,' he reflects. Some of his histrionic leanings found satisfaction on the pocket-sized stage where emotions were released and larger-than-life performances given. A keen company, an expectant audience – what more could a producer want?

Along with this, though, the same springs of feeling, allied to keen thinking, and rather differently directed, infused the local preaching that occupied some of his Sundays. At first he travelled with a senior and fully accredited local preacher, who kept an avuncular eye on the fledgling, and critically followed the small part in the service allotted to the 'new boy'. Then ensued a period 'On Trial', and finally George found himself 'On Full Plan'. Then began a lifetime of climbing up pulpit steps that was to take him into tiny village chapels, into the Central Hall at Tonypandy, proprietorial in its warmth and affection, and ultimately to a crowded ecumenical congregation in Llandaff Cathedral. At the beginning, though, it was hard work, for the short hour in front of the congregation had to be backed by the necessary hard grind of study. And there was other homework to be covered too, the passing of vital exams that would send him from the Grammar School to University College, Southampton.

In the Sunday school class which he led, he found that he could be useful, and possessed the ability to talk to the young-sters, getting on to their level, and drawing out a satisfying response. He found, in effect, that he could teach, and made up his mind at last that this would be a good career for every day. He decided to become a schoolmaster, and after University and training, went to his first school in a tough district of South London, known locally as the Elephant and Castle.

He had made the breakaway from his Valleys and was on the road to becoming world-minded, an aspect of his personality that must soon strike anyone who really listens to him talking. Yet the extensive travels that have taken him in later years to Finland, Africa, Russia, North and South America, Greece, Poland, Czechoslovakia and Jugoslavia, often on parliamentary missions, were still a very long way off. He smiles now as he remembers that, until he was twenty-four years old, he had made only one visit to London.

The children south of the Thames who were his first teaching charge may have seemed in some ways rather different from the boys and girls of his own environment, but he rapidly came to terms with them.

Probably he soon realized that they had their own frustrations to contend with, and little of the natural beauty of the Valleys for compensation. Teaching was in itself full of fascination and his chosen career appeared thoroughly satisfying.

There was also time off, even for a super-conscientious schoolmaster and, in moments of relaxation, the young man made his way round the metropolis; it was bound to be full of attractions, as the greatest city in the world. Inevitably, with his keen political interests, he was drawn to the Mother of Parliaments. Here was Westminster, as he had always imagined it, thronged by a cosmopolitan crowd; here was Big Ben, as he gazed up, and there the River Thames flowing alongside. As he paused outside the famous grey buildings, wondering about the events that took place inside, he day-dreamed of what he would do if ever he were a member of that august body. Well, there was nothing to stop him from joining the public as a sightseer. He attached himself to the slowly moving queue and eventually found himself inside the historic portals. Here was a whole new world, to set the pulse racing. Yet he emphasizes now that, at the time, he would have been incredulous at the idea of ever sitting in the House.

'Later,' he says, 'doors opened for me, and others came

forward and persuaded me to go ahead; from then onwards, doors of service seemed to be always opening. . . .'

But this was still all a long way off, and would have appeared as an unattainable vision to the young teacher still finding his feet in a strange new city.

Meanwhile, not only teaching itself delighted him, but the status and interests of his profession concerned him increasingly; he simply could not resist opportunities to involve himself in teachers' well-being. As time passed, he returned to Wales and taught in schools in Cardiff. Here also he became President of the Cardiff Class Teachers' Association, where his abilities as a speaker, and now as administrator too, flourished. He was elected as President of the Cardiff Association of the N.U.T. and for five years served on the National Executive of the Union, since 1945 being one of the Union's Parliamentary representatives.

In spite of his absorption in his chosen profession and an increasing public life, political interests continued to dominate; he could no longer ignore either his own inner promptings nor the persuasions of other people. He was compelled to face the possibility of another and larger destiny. Doors opened to admit him to Westminster and in 1945 he took his seat as the Member for Cardiff Central.

He says that he does not believe in allowing an opportunity to pass by, but tries to seize it. 'Saying "No" is not my philosophy!' he declares roundly.

Over twenty years have passed since that time, but those early days are not likely to be forgotten; finding his way round the rambling corridors of the House, taking in his stride the ancient customs still persisting, making his maiden speech, and getting to know the personalities of the House – everything was fascinating. He was youthful enough to be full of enthusiasm, and zeal. This he would even now consider absolutely essential.

'To be effective in party politics, youngsters coming in must be ON FIRE!' he asserts, and he himself, through the preliminary stages of his parliamentary career and during the ensuing years also, has never lost the early flame.

Young enough for contemporary thinking, old enough for a

mature judgement, there was one other quality that characterized George Thomas on entering Parliament which was there even beforehand, and which has endured. His capacity for sheer hard work is a by-word. Some have said that he drives himself almost beyond the limits of his physical stamina; certainly he does not spare himself. Recalling now the concentrated study and dedication of his youthful years, he indicates that youngsters who want to make a contribution to society must expect these tensions.

'. . . they must accept the necessary discipline and hard work and long hours, but they will get a tremendous kick from it'. There is no doubt at all that in saying this he reflects his own experience, not only in the political sphere, but in the service of his church as well.

In 1950, he was returned for Cardiff West, which he has represented ever since. He won a secure place in the esteem of members of all parties; it has been said that he has 'strong convictions but no enemies'. He himself feels that, in some ways, those in politics are faced with fewer challenges than people in other spheres, since the House of Commons, he thinks, is quick to respect the religious convictions of its members when these are plainly and unequivocally held and demonstrated.

Office followed and experience was gained in the Ministry of Civil Aviation and other posts. Then, as Minister of State for his native land, he could now effectively serve Wales in a capacity that gave him infinite quiet pride. Could he not remember the endless debates of the Mission 'Men's Parliament', the opinions of various shades and force that had been thrust upon him during his many years of public life? Now, in so far as was constitutionally possible, he would do what he could for the land and the people so dear to him.

Not that he intended to look backwards, or inwards, to the era of tall pointed hats, shawls and spinning-wheels! Wales possessed great natural beauty, no one can deny, and her romantic charm is a palpable tourist attraction, but there was so much more than this. Moreover, by strengthening her links with the West of England, she could greatly benefit by a more outward-looking attitude. All this he firmly believed.

His engagement diary became crowded. Nor did the Minister of State for Wales cease to maintain his Methodist ties; he was forced to curtail his preaching, but still prepared carefully the sermons that he preached three or four times a quarter. He regarded, as he still does, his links with the local church as absolutely vital – 'one's life-line', as he says. The balance is hard to achieve, he thinks, but essential for successful living. His devotion to his spiritual roots was publicly and warmly acknowledged by his election to the Vice-Presidential Chair of the Methodist Conference, a position this body affords to distinguished laymen and women.

He has occasionally been criticized for the major place Methodism holds in his affections, but he remains steadfast in his allegiance. During a triumphant year of Vice-Presidency, he gave prodigally of his energies and time to serve the church that so honoured him. He had not married; during these hectic days, he must have reflected that this particular freedom was then, at any rate, a considerable advantage! All along the line, though, he was supported by his 'Mam', who was quietly thrilled with her son's acclamation.

Speaking to George Thomas now, one is conscious of a man of slight build, youthfully energetic despite the grey wavy hair; he is bright-eyed, affable and unassuming, but with his own quiet authority, and extremely alert. He speaks very fluently and with much conviction, and his phraseology is colourful, the fine hands emphasizing his opinions. He has by no means lost touch with young people and cares deeply that they should be concerned with world affairs.

'If democracy is to survive, we must have young people taking an interest in politics; the parties need their idealism and moral courage of their beliefs, and Christian convictions . . . if they avoid this, the field is left clear for others who have no such convictions; the young then abrogate their right to speak on moral issues, such as Vietnam, and the care of the aged. . . .'

Asked if he thought this viewpoint was put over firmly

enough by the church, he confessed to thinking it is done in a rather 'patchy' manner. Many ministers of religion, he believes are afraid – and to his mind falsely – of 'losing' promising youngsters from organized church activities. As a young fellow, he was himself once 'put off' in this way, but he simply cannot understand any such dichotomy of emphasis. He agrees that there is an inevitable tension in reconciling church work and political life, but it is possible to resolve such a situation to a considerable degree, he argues.

As a Free-Churchman he cannot but notice the comparative absence of Nonconformists in public life at the present time. All Christians, in fact, he believes, face the temptation to be too inward-looking and must stir themselves to take their place in local government, on the bench, and similar activities. He is emphatic in his conviction that church members should more and more occupy the citadels of power in the country.

'Of course there is a great enthusiasm among youth for good causes,' he readily agrees, 'but young people must realize that the most vital way of helping the under-privileged is by having a real voice in the places of power!' He does not decry the energy and goodwill put by youngsters, many still in their teens, into 'good cause' ventures, recalling with some humour his own 'agreement' to undertake four miles in the Cardiff 'Oxfam' Walk – 'my four miles surely equals their greater efforts!'. . . .

Here is a man who has now become accustomed to position and authority, yet whose genial personality still commands not only respect but much affection. An Anniversary at the Central Hall of his old home-town, Tonypandy, brings him a 'surging tide' of response. In his constituency, he seems to have friends everywhere. His infectious charm is able to penetrate the seemingly impervious. Kenneth Greet, a Methodist minister formerly stationed at Tonypandy, tells one story of these disarming powers at work.

Mr. Greet was sitting with the new Vice-President in an hotel lounge, where the only other occupant was a rather frigid Englishman, firmly entrenched behind his newspaper. With typical good-humour, George Thomas tried to draw the stranger into conversation, a gambit at first meeting with little success. Reluctant monosyllables only were the response.

'Do you come from Wales?'

'No! . . .'

'Ah, a pity . . . where from then?'

. . . 'Hull'.

'Spelt with a "u" or an "e"?'

'A "u" . . .'

Are you a Methodist by any chance?'

'No! . . .'

'Oh, I think you'd better become one then, or else it might be spelt with an "e"! . . .'

The absurdity of this situation finally conquered the stranger's resistance; he lowered his newspaper and was forced to smile.

Here is not only an important Welshman but increasingly a figure on the larger scene, who puts his abilities to use where-ever they are required.

'When I was young,' he says, 'the church was a driving force for social justice; nowadays it is not so easily seen that we not only need a welfare state, but also a welfare world . . .'

In other words, we should be constantly looking outwards. This is undoubtedly true of George Thomas. It is perhaps fitting that he should later transfer to further Government office as the Minister of State for Commonwealth Affairs, and be proud to serve under-privileged peoples. Being what he is, he could never spend his entire life, physically, spiritually, or politically, on one side only of the Severn Bridge. And he is still exceedingly youthful in outlook. . . .

6

The Challenge of 'Hattie'

MICHAEL COBB

'All precautions should be taken . . . Hattie is now making for the coast, near Belize . . . winds are 150 to 200 miles an hour, with a following tidal wave of 15 feet. . . .' The radio announcement ended.

The date was Monday, the 30th of October, well on in the hurricane season of the Caribbean. Only the day previously, Hattie had been making herself felt out at sea, apparently heading for Jamaica and Cuba. It is the habit of hurricanes to follow the path of the prevailing wind and it had become clear that this one might easily get into the path of the North-east Trades and come straight for British Honduras. The terse statement from Belize radio now confirmed that this was indeed happening.

Local people did not need to be told what this meant. Without wasting time on words, they hurried about their affairs, the only too familiar business of preparing to sit-out the violence of the hurricane's visitation; there was nothing to be done actually to prevent its inevitable onslaught. In Belize City they scuttled about moving belongings from ground floors to higher and safer quarters, or battened them down, and effected such reinforcements as were possible to try to stem the anticipated ordeal. The old and the very young, and those living dangerously near to water levels, made arrangements to go to the specially strengthened shelters, good solid buildings of concrete and cement, that were provided for them. With a certain fatalism, they did what they could.

For those present who were not Hondurans, who had never undergone these hazards, it was an even more disturbing experience. Michael, and the other V.S.O. personnel from

Wesley College, braced themselves for the duties ahead. They had some idea, from hearsay, of the tasks before them, but the prospect was unnerving, to say the least. These young cadet teachers from England were all set to make themselves as useful as possible and, accepting the value of easy identification, they changed into scout gear. Everyone knew that the scouts were on duty at official shelters during these crises and would naturally turn for help to the familiar uniform.

About midday, Wesley College closed its doors and the Government carpenters came and boarded up all the windows. Michael went off to his allotted post at the Wesley Primary school, his heart beating rather faster than usual. Throughout his preparations, the radio announcer had continued with instructions to the general public, stating which shelters were already full, and reminding them of the urgency of storing food, water and kerosene oil, for the siege ahead. All day the activity continued. There was a feeling of tension and the air was hot and still and menacing. Michael was able to get back to the college for some food and, in view of the threat of the expected tidal wave, he took his own personal belongings to the first floor, to which the Principal and his family had removed, the house being as nearly indestructible as possible. After a good meal, Michael went off again to his duty post. There was little to do but wait. Hattie was reported to be approaching relentlessly on her predestined route.

As the minutes ticked by, the occupants of the shelter grew restless and apprehensive. The young man thought over this unenviable position and the reason why he himself was right in the middle of it. 'Voluntary Service Overseas' – this was the official title of the organization under whose auspices he had come to Central America only a month or so earlier. Less well known at this time, V.S.O. had been formed a few years before with three objectives; to help the developing nations to solve their economic, technical and educational problems, to improve relationships and break barriers by providing a field in which young people from different environments might work together, and to give these young people an opportunity to widen their own sympathies and understanding through service overseas. During his last term at his public school, Michael had listened to a speaker presenting the case for V.S.O. and the idea of volunteering had taken hold of him.

He admitted to himself that his motives for volunteering had been mixed; he would not deny to himself that he had been attracted by the chance of travelling, leaving the cocoon of home and family, meeting interesting people and taking the plunge into a more adventurous way of life. National Service having ended, here was a splendid setting in which to find one's feet in an adult world. Were these selfish reasons? He supposed they were, to some extent. Yet, beneath all this, but strongly propelling him forwards, as he had completed forms and supplied particulars, was an awareness of a genuine desire to meet the challenge of such a venture. Here was a chance to use his expensive education and many advantages, just for a short spell, to help others less fortunate. There was, he supposed, no one clear reason why he had put forward his name, but the mixture of reasons certainly included a real wish to extend himself in a testing situation, and give back some of the benefits he had received. Delightful, church-going parents, a happy family life, he possessed all these. V.S.O. would offer a clear-cut field of service in which he could demonstrate some gratitude before life's inexorable claims gripped him.

At school, he was the first to admit, he had not counted himself as particularly academic, though he was intelligent enough. Always a keen out-of-doors man, he had thrown himself with zest into all forms of sport, finding special pleasure in rugger, squash and cricket. He was fond of music too, playing in the school orchestra, in the military band, and enjoying himself in contemporary fashion in the pop group. With the vigour and assurance of youth, he had liked to hold his own in the debating society and had found a quiet satisfaction in the Bible-study group running at school. Taking it all round, life was pleasant, he had thought, and he hoped it would continue so. Surely V.S.O. would prove yet another fascinating experience, and a fellow such as himself could fit in reasonably well.

To his gratification, he had been accepted as a cadet teacher, and on leaving school found himself appointed to the staff of

Wesley College, Belize, in British Honduras; here he was to act as games master. The necessary briefing completed, he had made the journey to Central America, a flight all too quickly over. He recalled the white airport buildings at their destination, attractive with flowers and creepers, and the journey into Belize City; the road had passed partly through the countryside and partly alongside the river. He had noticed a saw-mill, sawing mahogany as he afterwards learned; there were several agreeable country houses built on stilts and painted in gay colours; there were the glorious flowering trees, vivid against the blue sky. They had crossed the swing-bridge over the Belize River, and skirted many fine Government buildings. About five minutes later, they had reached Wesley College, on the lagoon.

Michael had found a home from home with the Principal of the College, a fine Jamaican Christian and his warm-hearted and motherly wife, a British Honduran by birth. Independence, he had reflected, was all very fine in its way, but the free, happy atmosphere of his new home had won his allegiance straight away. There were companions also, other Volunteers sharing his lodgings, with whom to enjoy this new and interesting existence. As well as superintending games, he had been asked to teach some other subjects, including English language and literature. This had not proved too easy, but he had applied himself whole-heartedly to this challenge and had found, as the days passed, that his confidence grew.

Any 'race barriers' that might have existed were soon broken through and he found a great liberation in this fellowship of varied nationalities. His pupils at Wesley College were mostly Creole, a mixture of European and African descent. He found them just as endearing and exasperating as children anywhere, with a gaiety and good-humour that helped to make the work enjoyable. Outside the life of the College, he made other contacts; he met a few Spanish people, Indians and Caribs too. Human relationships had always seemed comparatively easy and he had quickly made friends and formed acquaintances. He had joined the local Scout troop and thrown himself with enthusiasm into the movement. Getting down to the job, and thoroughly enjoying his leisure in this unusual setting, he had hardly noticed that a month had soon flown by.

Suddenly, he had realized the existence of the one threat that was never far from the consciousness of the people. From July until October or early November, they could never be sure of remaining unmolested by the terrible hurricanes that menaced the island-studded Caribbean and the Honduran coast, bringing misery and desolation in their watery wake. Snatches of conversation, anecdotes overheard, visible evidence of past damage, had all forced on him the precarious nature of life under the shadow of nature at its most furious. Some of the local people remembered only too well the fearful storm of 1931, when a tidal wave had engulfed Belize and one hundred and fifty lives had been lost. He had not realized before how sinister these visitations could be. And now, awaiting the arrival of this predatory female – 'Hattie' as she had been named – he knew that he himself would be in the thick of such a situation, sharing with other people in the Colony all the dangers that lay ahead, that they had such cause to fear. He was relieved that he had been given a job to do, and that he was young and fit enough to be of some possible use.

Michael was interrupted in these reveries; as time had passed, the wind had risen. By ten o'clock the rain had started pouring down and by one o'clock in the morning, the radio had gone off the air. Another hour or two passed and Hattie was now in full swing. It was impossible to shut out the frightful roar of the wind and rain and the creaking and groaning of roofs and buildings, followed by dismaying thuds as they crashed to the ground. Within the shelter, even those who were used to these events could not pretend to be unaffected; the noise outside was so terrifying. Some found the experience hard to bear and were visibly upset; one or two women moaned, children whimpered. To his relief, Michael found that he was able to help considerably in calming the more nervous among them. His ability to get on well with people was of the utmost value here and he discovered that a confident manner and ready smile, a joke here and there, went a long way in encouraging others to a similar composure. Easily recognizable in his scout's uniform, he strolled around the shelter, giving a cheery word, reassuring the mothers, little children and old people, having no time at all to think of danger to himself. It was undoubtedly an alarming experience, even for the most robust, but he schooled himself to try to dismiss the battery of sound on the other side of the walls, and to concentrate on keeping up the spirits of those who, with him, waited for Hattie to pass on and leave Belize. He did not think of himself as a marvellously successful Christian, but he was aware of inner spiritual strength that reinforced his natural youthful vitality and courage.

At last daylight came, and with it a slight easing of the wind; the hurricane had gone full circle and was now nearly back to its starting-point. He made a quick reconnaissance outside; the air was foul, which was not surprising, when he considered the scene of appalling desolation that met his eye, the mud and debris everywhere. Everything unfortunate enough to stand in the hurricane's path had received a fearful battering; roofs had been torn off, trees plucked out as if by giant hands, and tossed around like matchsticks. And worse was to come, for after the wind, came the water. To places near the sea, lagoon and river, a solid wall of chilling grey water, ten feet or more high, swept along, shovelling all before it. Further inland, broken by the strong buildings, the water swished around the shelters to the height of about three feet, dirty and depressing, as it oozed through the ground-floor dwellings and snaked about the streets. At its most extreme, the water caused as much danger as the hurricane that preceded it, but by ten o'clock in the morning, it seemed to be retreating and the people could begin to feel safe. Now was the moment of ghastly truth; as they crept out, they surveyed the damage and began to assess the situation, and to rescue casualties.

During these difficult days, the V.S.O. fellows showed their mettle. Scouts were asked to co-operate in emergency action with the police, and with British and American service personnel. Human beings were of more value than property and immediately a search was made, both to recover the bodies of those killed in the disaster, and for injured people who might be unable to make their own way to First Aid Posts. With his companions, Michael set out to take part in the search. Death in this dramatic manner was something he had not faced before, and it was no light ordeal for a young man to seek out the fatally injured in this way and reverently help the police on the silent return journey.

In the more isolated areas, they sometimes found people who had been hurt and were waiting desperately for transport. Unfortunately, there was so much wreckage strewn about that vehicles could seldom be used and they just had to figure out some way of getting the badly wounded to medical aid. It also needed some ingenuity to persuade some of the victims to co-operate. Often in a state of shock, tearful and frightened by all that had happened, they became a little obstinate, and made things difficult for themselves and their rescuers. Michael, with his attractive smile and friendly manner, scored here; he seemed to have the knack of soothing the hysterical and producing co-operation. They found one old woman still shrinking away in a crumbling building, too nervous to come out. Through the dust and rubble they fought their way to her and gently inspected her badly bruised leg. Though not seriously hurt, she obviously required attention at the First Aid Post and had to be lured there somehow. At first, she flatly refused to move off, muttering to herself and sobbing, determined to stay exactly where she was. Patiently, Michael coaxed and pleaded; after all, she had to be treated like a frightened child.

'Come on, Granny, you'll be O.K . . . She looked up at the smiling face and relaxed a little, even achieving a smile herself. Perhaps it would be better to go off with this young chap, he seemed to know what he was about, and looked strong and capable . . . still a bit reluctant, she allowed herself to be gently helped outside. Soon, she was receiving medical care at the F.A.P., safe in the hands of a competent and understanding staff. With a grin to himself, Michael left the old lady talking volubly, pouring out her pent-up feelings, and went off in search of other victims of Hattie's cruelty. At least that duty had ended happily!

A couple of days of bright sunshine followed, a great blessing, and the V.S.O.s worked untiringly, keeping up morale wherever they went, in scenes of the utmost desolation. Michael felt deeply involved in the plight of the Honduran people and scarcely realized how short a time he had actually spent with them. These terrible experiences united human beings very tightly in a common bond of disaster. He found himself feeling keenly on behalf of those who were bereaved, or had suffered injuries, or the loss of their homes and belongings. How much he respected and admired their courage and endurance! There was no doubt about it, he might have come to British Honduras as a schoolboy, but the events of the last few days had turned him into a man.

He became unpleasantly aware that all was not right with him and that he was feeling very peculiar indeed. It soon dawned on him, in his feverish state, that he was going down with some kind of illness. He had certainly felt tired – looking back, he knew they had all worked without stopping while the need was the greatest, but this was different. What a time to be ill! No time for delay; he hurried off to the M.O. who diagnosed a touch of dysentery and gave appropriate directions. Gloomily, Michael obeyed. There was still so much to do. However, to his relief, prompt treatment paid off and he made a quick recovery.

By now, worried V.S.O. parents in England had heard all about Hattie, and subsequent events. Well-intentioned letters arrived at Belize, suggesting that offspring should return home to more stable climes. There were some raised eyebrows and shaken heads among the Volunteers. Parents! Didn't they grasp that this was no time to disappear! They meant well, of course, but V.S.O. personnel were not kids . . . dutifully, the letters were answered and it was emphasized, kindly but firmly, that all Volunteers were in good shape and could not possibly leave just now. They hoped relations would understand. Michael, subject understandably to just such correspondence, wrote to his father and mother stating that the Principal of Wesley College intended to re-start the school soon, in spite of the loss of four classrooms and their equipment. Michael was most anxious, as he pointed out, to give a hand here and wanted to stay a little longer.

He set about the task confronting the College authorities. The school furniture had been carried away in a fantastic fashion by the tidal wave. Happily, as though tracking a gold vein, people came running in to report sight of desks, tables and chairs, which floated into their ken in an inconsequential manner. From all parts of the city, articles were retrieved and triumphantly returned to refurnish what might have been described as merely 'teaching space'. Gradually, equilibrium was achieved, and life returned to normal. The year came to an end and the horrors of Hurricane Hattie faded away. Michael was pleased at the progress of the cricket team, whose fortunes he had sought to improve. To his satisfaction, they retained the Inter-Schools Cup. Not a major triumph, perhaps, but the outcome of hard work and encouragement.

At the end of twelve months service, Michael knew that, however reluctantly, he must go back to England. He felt that he had been accepted, not only by the school, but in the life of the Colony. His short term of V.S.O. duty had proved infinitely more engrossing – and exciting – than anything he could have imagined. It would certainly seem pretty tame and ordinary back in England; it was good-bye now to the sunshine and the many friends he had made.

It did in fact take some time to become used again to normal home life, pleasant though it was to see one's family again, and to find this reaction mutual – they had really missed him! It was a grind at first to settle down and begin work in an office, so far from the colourful background he had become accustomed to. Gradually, the adjustment was made, and he decided to try to find some way of continuing in the V.S.O. spirit. Spells of duty at the local Cheshire Home supplied such an opportunity and there were happy hours spent in the company of those who, in spite of being hampered in life's race, set an example of brisk non-despair. He appreciated the warm welcome of these bracing new acquaintances.

Sometimes too he would be invited to talk to school audiences of youngsters in their late teens, to put over to them some of the appeal and challenge of V.S.O. 'There is so much to say, I could go on for a forty-minute lecture!' he had joked, but it was true. Perhaps one could never find the words for such an experience.

A few years have gone by now, with many events crowding in. But Michael can still speak with enthusiasm of his V.S.O. days. 'For me,' he says, 'it was undoubtedly the best year I have ever spent. I just hope I gave the people I met something in return for the wealth of experience, understanding and happiness which I received. . . .'

He adds: '. . . if anyone has the chance, however small, and the desire, however weak, to do V.S.O. work, then they should seriously do all they can to take it. . . .'

V.S.O., with its headquarters in London, is now a widely-known feature of the modern scene. Most Volunteers, it seems, would second Michael in his appreciation of this imaginative form of social service. In an increasing number of spheres – educational, agricultural, medical and technical–graduate and qualified Volunteers, and Cadets also, go overseas, both giving and receiving in the process. For young Christians, such as Michael, it can provide a most congenial and challenging experience.

7

Sunday Revolutionary

H. A. HAMILTON

Here is a cheerful scene; there are mothers and fathers, grand-parents and cousins, aunts and uncles. Also, beside them, as in most gatherings, there are the little 'steps and stairs' that make up the rising generation. They are obviously all engaged in some absorbing activity, and a happy one at that. There are, to be honest, the occasional whispers, a giggle or two, the dropping of various objects, and one cannot deny that sense of perpetual motion that rightly characterizes any group where normal children are present. Movement is undoubtedly in the air, but it is the wind of progress. There is a surge of vitality about this crowd of people; they are very much alive.

Perhaps surprisingly, this wideawake and lively group is not watching an entertainment, but taking part in an act of worship. They are not an audience, but a congregation. The hard pews of the average church might seem an unlikely focus for revolution, yet in just such pews some striking changes have been taking place during the last few years. Because of this, more and more church services now give the appearance of one large Family. Older members are lovingly tolerant and interested in younger members, not expecting them to understand all that goes on, but remembering effectively that they are there! So, in spite of the small figures, the childish voices, the lively limbs, there is a great and awesome atmosphere of Oneness, and of reverence too. In the litanies and short prayers and other acts of worship prepared for them, the children join their elders.

At first, the smallest have found some difficulty in putting their minds to this, but as the weeks have passed, their confidence has grown. Even the smallest shows some awareness of

E

his or her rightful place in God's House, with the others of God's family, those grown-ups who sing so heartily at their sides. And when it is time for them to go to another part of the building, for group activity specially suited to their age, they skip off purposefully but with enough discipline.

Some of the very little ones look up shyly as they pass, waving to the tall figure in the pulpit, whom they now know as their priest or minister. One or two of the bolder spirits give him a broad grin, while one five-year-old has even been known to include him in a conspiratorial wink. Irreverent? The minister does not think so. He is delighted that the children know him by sight, and, while respecting him, look to him as the big friend he wishes to be.

The pioneering of this Sunday Revolution has been largely the work of one man. H. A. Hamilton has spent a lifetime in Christian education, working concentratedly at methods of communicating the knowledge and experience of the faith, particularly among the young. An ordained minister of distinction of the Congregational Church, he has never ceased caring about the spiritual welfare of the future generation. Nor has he stopped insisting that others should share his own concern.

'I do not think, even now, that the church is interested in its children to the extent of costly care,' he asserts firmly. 'Wrestling with this idea', as he puts it, has underlain the many years of thought and experiment from which evolved his vision of the 'Family Church'. Actively persuading church members to accept the responsibility of the whole church for its young people and winning their co-operation, along with that of Sunday school staff, has proved gruelling. Yet it has proved a challenge to which this robust pioneer has been serenely equal. Many churches now participating in some form of Family Church can scarcely recall a time when things were different, so familiar to them has this pattern become. But it was not always so.

H. A. Hamilton has viewed the business of Christian education from many angles, academic and practical; certainly it can never be said of him that he has looked at it only from within an ivory tower. At the very outset of his own adult life, the commonsense attitude of his father put him on a path for which he has ever since been grateful. Before going to theological college, on which he had set his heart, the young graduate of Manchester University was encouraged to go into business for a spell. This, as he now emphasizes, gave a 'sort of direction' to his thinking, and convinced him that 'the presentation of religion must be in terms of the experience of people outside the church to meet the needs of people inside the church'. These years taught him that 'theology is only true as you see it at work in the lives of people'. Having grasped these basic insights early in life, he has never fallen into the trap of mere theorizing, in however intellectual a framework such theorizing might be set. This emphasis was confirmed at his theological college where, wisely, as he considers, the young ministers in embryo were trained to be 'men first, and students second'.

Thus sensibly equipped, he went to his first pastorate, after his ordination in 1924. This charge, in Lancashire, was 'a great formative experience'. This he agrees with some laughter, reflecting that in the strange new world of mills and foundries he had needed to be 'thoroughly taken in hand'. The young people of his church soon let him know that he had still much to learn; they admitted him to their fellowship with a warmth that enveloped him and gave him confidence. These lassies and lads were not, for the most part, academic types, but their innate 'horse-sense' and truly fine qualities proved unexpectedly challenging. He found that he was forced to re-examine the accepted statements of the church as to its social witness, and found some of these statements hoary rather than useful.

For example, the concept of 'doing one's best in one's daily job' had surely been over-simplified; in the life of the mill, intense effort might simply put more money in employers' pockets, but not prove very gainful to the workers . . . All this was rather puzzling at first to the idealistic young minister, and many familiar tenets had to be re-appraised in the light of the concrete situations he was meeting day by day. He came to admire the boys and girls of the district and to feel a growing kinship. He had enjoyed a good family life himself, as a boy, and the stimulating companionship of his tough young Lancashire contemporaries was invigorating.

He was also fascinated by the extraordinary Sunday school 'his' church possessed. This was an Edwardian-type structure, of about seven hundred and fifty scholars of varying ages. Arrayed in rows, in the manner undeniably of an earlier era, instruction was somewhat crude in method, yet there was a real solidity of learning throughout the whole age-range. It dawned upon him that they were learning like a very large but genuine family-group, and the teaching was effective! This school greatly impressed him and remained in his memory long after he had left the town and the church behind. This experience was the foundation of his subsequent and enduring emphasis on family worship and caring. He faced the fact that the values of separateness and of group-involvement must somehow be reconciled.

It was time to move, and in Birmingham he found even more rewarding contacts with young people. There were naturally more varied occupations in this larger city, and more varied were the needs of the teenagers and young adults. Opportunities were seized for them to develop a 'community sense'. 'Active service' gave the young people a sense of significance, of feeling that they mattered in the community. 'So often,' muses H. A. Hamilton, 'we ask of them substitute things, that are not of any interest to them, or value.' He proved to himself that they could be taken seriously; if the challenge to the young people was large enough, there was hardly any limit to what they might achieve.

Knowledge and experience continued to reinforce the ideas with which his mind bubbled. Others noticed his gifts with the younger generation, observed his ability to communicate and to get things done. They felt the force of the positive but pleasing personality, whom young folks could call 'friend' as well as Minister. It was not surprising, therefore, that the Congregational Union brought him out from his pastoral charge and made him their denominational Youth Secretary. For the following thirteen years, he abandoned himself to this specialized activity, and during this period, instituted experiments of great and far-reaching significance.

The first three years were spent, as he says, 'looking, and talking, and finding things out'. It is not for nothing that 'Who's Who' lists one of his recreations as 'conversation'; the didactic approach has never characterized H.A.H., and his ability to listen as well as to speak has brought its own rewards. In dialogue with youth workers of all kinds, he went on learning, and confirming opinions that he had himself held for a long time.

As he travelled around the country, visiting Sunday schools and youth organizations, he discovered, as he had expected, much dedicated and strenuous service; some of this was seen to be rewarded, but much was plainly frustrated, and the end product was disappointing. He confirmed what he had long suspected, that the separateness of much Sunday school organization was a source of weakness; many children scarcely felt that they belonged to their own church – the church which they saw, most probably, only once or twice during a whole year. Without any sense of 'oneness', it was hardly surprising that their hold on the church was slight, and they tended to drift off in their teens, just at the time when it was hoped they would find a fulfilling place in the church's life. It had been a case of 'us' in the Sunday school and 'them' in the church, and seldom did these twain meet.

His musings on the need for some change were reinforced by a current report from the Ministry of Education, concerning the way in which children learn. Stress was laid on the points that children learn most successfully from within themselves, and also that they absorb their standards from those of the community. Thinking about these facts in the light of the denominational situation, H. A. Hamilton made his own decision and formulated an experimental plan. The story of this plan, its inception and implementation, is told in his book *The Family Church*. Although it is now some years since this pioneering publication appeared, the book and the experiment it reported still count as a major influence in the development of Christian education.

As the author states, the success of the 'plan' depended entirely upon the willingness of 'sample schools' to co-operate with him. Fortunately, such co-operation was readily given. Admittedly, it took some time for some ministers and leaders to commend the scheme convincingly to their staffs and congregations, but the backing they eventually received encouraged them to go ahead.

Twenty-four 'experimental stations' were selected and they consented to take part in the project for a period of about three years. They were chosen to represent all types of Sunday school work. North, south, suburban, rural, industrial, seaside – these varied communities provided opportunities for dispassionate scrutiny of a most critical nature. They agreed to participate in the ideal of 'Family Church'; in a joint act of worship in church, adults and young people were to pray and praise together, and feel themselves truly 'members one of another', despite the differences in age. The family pew of past ages, for the moment non-existent, was to be re-created on an infinitely larger scale. Children whose own parents did not attend, were given a 'church friend', with whom they could sit. This scheme, in anticipation so disturbing to some adult worshippers, proved heart-warmingly satisfying. When, at the appropriate moment, the children left for their own specific training, this itself was arranged in a new and much more flexible style. This experimental plan was designed to retain the undoubted value of the graded system, so hardly fought for a little earlier, but to relate this with the utmost significance to the total worship of the church family.

Such a quiet revolution demanded much persuasion, advice, instruction. Tirelessly, H. A. Hamilton went around drawing others into the orbit of his own unquenchable enthusiasm. Gradually, the reports of the experiments came in, and brought their own rewards. It would be untrue to say that in every congregation, the change-over to Family Church was smooth and uneventful, neither was a solution to every difficulty immediately found. But the new family spirit was sharply felt in many churches, and a new joy infused the teaching staff, the congregations who were willing to be responsive, and the young people themselves. In this new 'belonging', there was often a new future for the whole church. 'Family Church' is still working itself out in many areas, varying its procedures with experience, refining original plans and schemes, and still giving a new impetus to Christian education throughout the country.

Immediately after the Second World War, H. A. Hamilton was given the opportunity to spread his store of knowledge and experience throughout a yet wider circle. As Principal of Westhill College, he confronted his students with the importance of training. As he now says, 'there was not much left of Westhill then'. The buildings had been used as hostel accommodation for day-school teachers. There now seemed to be a new wave of interest, and a fresh will to become equipped for the vital tasks ahead. His experience in training the youth leaders of the first post-war course emerged, it seems to him, as a national opportunity of the first magnitude. 'We trained,' he recalls, 'among day-school teachers and professional children's workers . . . it was a miniature comprehensive world, and we looked at the whole range of youth service.' Going along with current educational trends, there was a progress away from the old-fashioned lecture methods to the seminar method, with an emphasis on practical work. These nine years proved exhilarating, and the contact with these eager, seeking minds, humbling and challenging.

'I had a wonderful staff too,' he says. 'I suppose I persuaded them, and convinced them . . . anyway, they went along with me magnificently in these new ways. . . .'

Life was by no means lived entirely within Westhill's walls; valuable further experience was gained by sharing in the service of youth in Birmingham. An important survey produced about that time, entitled '74,000 Adolescents', confirmed the Principal's long and strongly held conviction that 'social involvement is a necessary part of training'.

Suddenly, H.A.H. realized that he had been talking about education for twenty-two years. As he now says somewhat wryly, he decided to 'expose himself to the risk of a call'; plunging back into the ministry, he was given charge of a church in Brighton, then as now, a seaside town surging with varied youthful activity. In his church, he naturally enthused about Family Church, and his members trusted him, as he puts it, to make the morning service into one of his own pattern, using his favourite small prayer-book in which all could so readily and happily join.

He soon discovered, however, that much useful work was to be done again at ground level. Serving on the East Sussex and Brighton Education Committee and as Chairman of an Enquiry Committee into 'Youth in Brighton', he found life as fully absorbing and demanding as ever. As he looks back, H. A. Hamilton reflects, like many another active Christian, that 'one stage leads wonderfully to another'. In Brighton, he discovered, more forcibly perhaps than hitherto, the world of unattached youth, with its problems, maddening frustrations, and immense need. How much we can learn from social contacts, he repeats, and emphasizes his conviction that the young do need the concern and friendship of older people to give them a much-required security.

During his time at Brighton, the Congregational Union conferred a signal honour on this pioneer, by making him Chairman of the Union, bringing extra duties and considerable travelling. There were also the marked rewards of meeting fellow-churchmen throughout the Union, and receiving the affection of members everywhere.

Retiring from Brighton, at a time when perhaps some men would have thought of 'taking things more easily', H.A.H. found himself living in the beautiful Swiss city of Geneva, looking outwards in the most up-to-date ecumenical fashion. A period as Assistant General Secretary of the World Council of Churches utilized his considerable administrative gifts and brought him into contact in the most interesting way with Christians of all races and denominations, with their varying traditions. He implies that this was very salutary, as well as fascinating; one was forced to re-think, he suggests, the differences between prejudice and principle, on social matters. One needed to accept with tolerance the very different standards to be found even within the fellowship of Christians from other parts of Europe. At a conference, he remembers, there was one man who found it difficult to contemplate with equanimity the vision of H.A.H. dancing with his wife . . . Geneva was a great forum for concentrating on essentials.

'Bert' Hamilton, as his friends affectionately know him, can look back on much that is satisfying and enduring. And there are also what he terms the 'undeserved rewards'. Travelling around the British Isles, he may well meet someone from a former pastorate, or a practitioner in experimental youth work, eager to enter into dialogue. Even more thrilling are the occasions, often in the most unlikely places, when he is approached by men and women from the younger countries who greet him warmly and introduce themselves. Quite often they turn out to be former Westhill students, anxious to renew their acquaintance and acknowledge a genuine indebtedness to their student days and to the influence of their former Principal. A conference in Japan, a few years ago, proved to be a delightful reunion of erstwhile world-students of the College. A handsome Nigerian, smiling broadly, hurried up . . . he was now highly placed in the social service of his country.

'To meet such men and women is the greatest possible thrill', says the quiet revolutionary contentedly. Just one of the thrills, probably, of a stretch of years in constant contact with tomorrow's generation, sharing and reflecting their needs, their hopes and their vitality. . . .

8

Undefeated

CELIA PROPHETT

Three weeks after entering University, Celia Prophett awoke one October Saturday morning to find that fate had dealt her a cruel blow. Stricken with serious illness, she spent seven weeks in the Royal Infirmary, where fellow-students visited her continually and the medical staff were understanding and co-operative. She returned home in November, though, to accustom herself to a life of apparent inactivity and seeming lack of purpose. During the six years between that moment of utter depression and the present time, she has fought and won the battle against self-pity, and crammed into her proscribed existence more positive achievements than many people manage in a lifetime.

Born during an air raid in 1940, Celia grew up in a happy family in the Potteries area of England, among the warm and friendly people of that district. A typical 'girl-next-door', she had set her sights on higher education and did well at school. Energetic by nature, and moved to outgoing occupations by her Nonconformist background, she found time to teach in her local Sunday school and to join in the activities of the Youth Group attached to her church. This fellowship was forward-looking, well in advance of contemporary practice, and was pioneering in social service fields, long before such work was commonly undertaken. The members at Temple Street had visited old people and hospital patients, and carried out interior decorating for the aged and needy. Scraping and sandpapering and slapping on paint proved a heady experience for keen teenagers delighting in their own youth and high spirits, and finding the joy of acceptance by those they served in this way was very satisfying. It was tough going sometimes, but infinitely rewarding. And they had the fun of going together on various assignments, making worthwhile relationships among themselves and enjoying each moment of these golden years.

In 1957, a visiting minister talked to the group about the movement known as International Voluntary Service for Peace. They were impressed, and several of the young people wanted to know more of what was involved. As an upshot, three of them volunteered for a spell of duty with the organization, and found themselves in European work camps. Celia was appointed to a camp in the French Alps, where recruits were asked to help in clearing a village recently devastated by floods. This proved a gruelling but valuable experience; unfortunately, it was terminated somewhat abruptly by an attack of dysentery which laid all workers low. In spite of this unlooked for and unpleasant interruption, the volunteers went home undaunted, feeling the richer for this wider knowledge of their world and its needs. They would repeat the operation, they decided.

For one of them at least, this proved impossible. Towards the end of her days at grammar school, Celia found she could not rely on her usual buoyant health. Distressing symptoms recurred and she was forced to consult her doctor, and in turn, a specialist. The illness was diagnosed and the medical men were non-committal. They recommended hospital treatment and advised postponement of her hard-won entry into Bristol University. A nineteen-year-old girl could not but take such a decision hardly and Celia withdrew, temporarily, into herself. Was this the radiant future she had looked forward to? Was all that study and grind wasted? Supposing she did not make a good recovery?

With the resilience of youth, she put such thoughts behind her and threw herself, during the winter of 1959–60, into an arduous programme of working and social activities. There was a spell as a student teacher in an infant school, and debating in the city Youth League with a rival club. She took part in the city Youth Competition and qualified to lead the city team in a national competition. This was exciting and her competence in these events encouraged her. Moreover, her regular responsibilities in the Sunday school and with the youth group still absorbed her for a good deal of her time and the fellowship of these activities prevented lonely and pointless brooding. She had no foreboding, though, of the despair she was soon to know. It had been thought possible for her to enter Bristol and begin her University course, and with the highest of hopes she had made the necessary preparations, said good-bye to her family and friends and set off gaily for this new adventure. Then, after only three weeks' insight into University life and cheerful companionship, the blow had fallen. This illness, with its accompanying restrictions, was apparently to condemn her to a life that was no life . . . who could be blamed for feeling bitter?

The friends who usually seem to come forward in such a crisis were not long in making an appearance. Everyone was eager to do something for Celia, but they knew that pity was not what she would want, and were diffident and uncertain how best to help. Two older people, whose influence and concern were to prove immeasurable, were boldly successful. The Chief Education Officer of her home town and his wife, Mr. and Mrs. Dibden, realized the vital necessity of providing Celia with occupation that would engage her active mind and not offend her sensibilities. They searched around for something suitable.

Meanwhile, somewhat ironically, Celia was getting ready to celebrate her twenty-first birthday. She had spent a short time in the west country on a course of rehabilitation and training intended to help her in the new restricted life she must lead now. She was in little mood really for the congratulations and well-wishing usually showered on young people when they attain their majority. Still, she could not rebuff acquaintances in their genuinely meant good intentions, and the celebration was duly observed. It was with no particularly cheerful outlook that the birthday-girl surveyed her future. Yet, with so much good-will to surround her, and the inner resources of a sincere religious faith to sustain her, she made her own secret affirmation. She just would not accept the limitations people were prescribing for her. Twenty-one was the exciting edge of life; well, she would plunge right in, in spite of everything!

Events moved swiftly. Mr. and Mrs. Dibden guided her into a job that seemed absolutely made for her. She was to train a team for the city's Public Speaking Competition. This was well within her scope. With thoroughness, she set about putting the team through their paces. They responded to her leadership and, to their mutual delight, won the competition. Celia went on to train other teams for the city Youth Debates League.

She needed to 'take in' as well as to give; the eager, active mind was hungry for further knowledge. In January 1962, through a contact in I.V.S., arrangements were made for her to go to first-year lectures at Keele University. Six useful months followed, by which time an opportunity had occurred for her to work as a part-time assistant to a speech therapist. This suited her admirably. During the following winter she again trained teams for public speaking and debates. By now she was becoming experienced in this routine, and could polish off the rough edges and bring out the finer points that would spell victory. She suddenly realized that, in spite of everything, life was very much worth while. She was in action again and working – earning her own living, like other responsible young adults. She was exultant. In time, she felt able to cope with longer hours, and the part-time job lengthened into a five-day working week. Despite her disabilities, she was valuable to employers.

She also found that not in spite of, but because of, these very disabilities, a whole new sphere of Christian service had opened to her. The stresses and strains of the last few years had made imperative spiritual resources of immense magnitude, and she had discovered that these were really available. All one had been taught in Sunday school and in church about the love and power of God was true; prayer could bring courage and hope. This was not only a matter of relief and joy to her, but could be a source of inspiration to others. This was gradually unfolded to her as she was invited, first to one meeting and then to another. Her gifts as a public speaker flowered and she found herself talking happily to varied audiences, to whom she could speak confidently of the grace of God as a quality she was herself experiencing and continuing to rely upon. She spoke to women in their afternoon meetings, to church mixed gatherings, and perhaps most testing of all, to those only slightly younger than herself, in the youth groups with which she was so familiar.

Finding herself capable, once she had adjusted to the disadvantages of her condition, she was again absorbed in the activities of a local church. She offered her services on the challenging ground of a new housing estate, full of young couples and lively children. There was a Brownie pack requiring assistance, and she would give a hand there. An Inters Youth Club, with some rowdy elements, proved rather too much to handle, but the determination to attempt the task was not lacking. Conscious of her natural endowments of voice and gesture, allied to good mental powers, and willing to extend her sphere of testimony, Celia asked to be accepted as a local preacher of her church, and began the appropriate study. This was not an easy matter for her, but with family help and much perseverance, she grasped the privilege of the pulpit, and started to equip herself for this strenuous and taxing vocation.

Others, further afield, had come to hear of this young woman's fight against personal disability, and publicity was inevitable. Thinking about it, Celia decided that she could perhaps make her witness in these new and unsought ways, and agreed to co-operate. An article by a famous journalist in a huge circulation weekly magazine for women entered countless homes; women of all ages sat quietly by their firesides reading of Celia's indomitable spirit. The BBC television cameras turned on her and pin-pointed this dark-haired girl of such compelling personality, in a programme entitled 'No Turning Back'.

The minister to her church had accompanied her to what could not but prove something of an ordeal. As preparations were made to film the feature, the parson and a member of the BBC staff chatted together. The former came away with the impression that a 'motive' was being probed for to account for the whole-hearted involvement in life of the young woman being filmed. He was also convinced that such 'motive' as there really was had not been truly understood.

'Her "motive" is quite simple,' says the Rev. Peter Bayley – 'she has a great love for her Lord and this gives her strength and hope and courage and enables her to love other people as she so obviously does. Her faith doesn't "play a part" in her life – it is the very basis on which her life is built.'

Celia has always enjoyed acting. The imaginative Mrs. Dibden, ever on the look-out for forms of self-expression for her young friend, formed a drama society, intriguingly named 'The Etceteras'. They were chosen to perform an excerpt from a translation of a famous Greek tragedy in the city Youth and Adult Drama Festival. Calmly calling for the seemingly impossible, she announced that Celia would be cast in the leading role. The presentation, despite the inexperience of some of the actors, gained a first-class award. In fact, the play attracted mention in the national press. For Celia, it was a moving moment. Dressed gracefully in the dignified, flowing robes of the period, her hair arranged in Grecian style, she exulted in the noble lines and deep emotions portrayed. Admittedly, it was a play for a minority audience, one would think, but all present applauded thunderously. Neither the greater part of these, nor the adjudicator, knew of the handicaps over which Celia had needed to triumph. Antigone has been called the most celebrated drama in all Greek literature, and its heroine, bearing the title name, a model of womanly self-sacrifice. Underlying the entire tragedy is the sublime idea of a higher unseen law ruling the destinies of men.

Only a few members of that audience knew of the personal tragedy clouding the life of their chief character. And they could only dimly comprehend the isolation and the darkness; for the Country of the Blind can be understood only by those who are forced to live there, and to try to delineate it from without is a pointless presumption. Celia Prophett crossed the barrier on that terrible morning in October 1960, when she awoke and turned, unavailing, to look at the time on the watch she could only feel. Yet her sightless world is one in which she still dares to live adventurously.

To the observer, she is a young woman suffering from disseminated sclerosis, who cannot see, and sometimes comes a cropper with a heavy fall; yet she is also the one ready to get herself, however awkwardly, around the estate delivering envelopes for charities! To the watcher at the Greek drama, she is a person, little more than a girl, who played the part of that doomed heroine. To those who really know Miss Prophett at close quarters, she is simply Celia, with the sense of humour, and no trace of bitterness, who possesses inner resources the ancient Greeks had never known. The love of the Lord Jesus Christ has upheld her from the day of her birth, and never more than since the day the darkness fell. . . .

9

West meets East

SUSIE YOUNGER

If you want to see Susie at work, you will need to fly half-way round the world. Here she lives in the land she has described as 'a beautiful country, an age-old civilization, with talented, sensitive people'. Hanguk, as its inhabitants call it, occupies a peninsula extending south from the east coast of Asia, between Japan and China. Political and military upheavals have caused its partition, around the thirty-eighth parallel, into the countries we now think of as the Korean People's Republic in the mountainous north and the Republic of Korea in the south. Winters are icy, with winds coming in across Siberia, but the summers are almost tropical.

It is somewhat ironical that one of the names for Korea means 'Land of the Morning Calm', for the country has been subject to disturbing outside pressures, and torn by civil war. When hostilities ceased in 1953, enormous problems were thrown up, one legacy comprising a stream of refugees from North Korea into the South, including tens of thousands of orphans.

Despite immense efforts devoted to reconstruction since those tragic days, South Korea remains very poor, and faces in acute form the difficulties typical of any developing country. Population pressures are great, and unemployment rife.

Since she went to South Korea in 1959, at the age of twenty-three, Susie has undergone an extraordinary identification. She speaks the language fluently – this partly resembles Japanese in grammar and syntax, but is very different in sound and vocabulary. She is even said to dream in Korean! But on a recent visit to her native England, she has been able to focus a spotlight on some of the frustrations of the cheerful people whom she has taken to her heart, and on the projects of the Susie Younger Korean Trust, the registered charity which collects funds on her behalf.

Inevitably, people wonder about her background. They are puzzled and intrigued as to the impulse that directed this Englishwoman of good family to a strange and remote life, so many miles from her family and girlhood friends. Perhaps those who know her personally are less surprised; they will long have accepted her as an unusual person, extremely independent in her thinking, with a colossal fund of energy to implement her radical ideas and decisions. No one denies that she is a formidable character, much in the tradition of those nineteenth-century pioneers who accomplished incredible good works through their personal qualities and won countless admirers in the process. Her own personality has been assessed as 'a unique combination of visionary dedication and tough common sense'. Yet this gay young woman, with the deep-set brown eyes and cheerful freckles, obviously draws forth not only respect but affection too.

Girlhood and growing-up for Susie meant 'loving parents, good education, a fun-filled and stimulating life'. The elder daughter of the Rt. Hon. and Mrs. Kenneth Younger, she went to a school with Quaker traditions, although she herself was not a believing Christian until her conversion just before she left school. At this time she was confirmed as an Anglican. Afterwards, she went up to Oxford; besides involving herself to the full in the life of the University and enjoying the companion-ship of her contemporaries, she was also thinking deeply about her religious convictions.

'I spent three years trying to discover in what form, and with what authority, Our Lord had founded His Church,' she says. However, Anglicanism was not to be her final spiritual home, and eventually she was received into the Roman Catholic Church. Unlike some articulate Christians, she does not ascribe her conversion to the Christian faith particularly to the influence of any specific friend or adviser; she states that 'reading the Gospels for the first time was, for me, a living meeting with Christ Himself'.

Further mental discipline lay ahead, at the London School of Economics, where she trained as a social worker. Then she accepted an invitation to go for an uncertain length of time as a lay-missionary to Taegu, the third largest city in South Korea.

Accompanied by a friend, she entered a strange land and a new existence. For a year, Susie taught English and French in college and, during this time, wrestled with the unfamiliar language. Gradually, the preliminary excitement of adjusting to this new and exhilarating pattern of living subsided. She began to make uncomfortable contrasts between her own comparatively pleasant standard of living and the social problems of many Koreans outside the college. She very much loved the land and the people and was dismayed at the poverty and the difficulties of those who tried hard to live honestly and at the same time support themselves and their families in a reasonable manner.

With such a direct person, her experiences led promptly to action. She and her friend grew aware, for instance, of the miserable situation of the shoe-shine boys. Work for them was scarce and they were frequently rounded up into gangs by older youths or young men and exploited. Some of them only nine or ten years old, these small boys, often orphans, were soon hopelessly caught in a near-criminal way of life. They could scratch only a bare living, anyway, and had hardly any alternative. The two girls' hearts went out to these boys, often made cunning and old before their time.

With characteristic drive and success, she enlisted the co-operation of Oxfam, who immediately bought a tumbledown house for which she had negotiated. Here, in the nearest approach to a real 'home' some of them had ever known, the shoe-shine boys were made welcome, and helped, slowly, to get other jobs. Not unnaturally, the leaders of one of the street-gangs, who had formerly employed these boys, resented the interference and some uncomfortable incidents ensued. (Once the house was broken into, and once a boy was forced to return to his gang.) However, as time passed, this minor harrying ceased. For the boys fortunate enough to find their way into

Susie's care, life began again. They were given training for jobs, to support themselves in the precarious economy, and thoroughly enjoyed the companionship of this stable home setting.

Two years later, the local government enlisted the help of the Catholic Church for girls who wanted to get out of prostitution. Inevitably, something had to be done for them and the Archbishop asked Susie to take on the job. So, as she is reported to have told a newspaper correspondent, she 'took a step deeper into the underworld' and challenged the evil men who made their living through the degradation of young womanhood.

No matter how eager girls might be to pursue honourable and productive employment, there was so little for them to do. Educational standards in Korea are high; difficulty arises later, when employment is sought. Apart from a tiny minority who find satisfactory posts, girls looking for jobs are faced with a big question mark. Naturally they hope to marry, but many need to work for a while at least, and the daughters of rural labourers in particular, anxious to help their hungry families, feel themselves under pressure to try and earn.

Susie found that girls from the country, as many have done before and since all over the world, left home to seek their fortune in the city. They might, to begin with, find themselves jobs as waitresses. Unfortunately, many encountered the 'talent scouts' of the vice-rings and found themselves eventually lured into brothels. Quickly indebted to the brothel-keepers for small sums of money, they soon experienced the turn of the screw, and only the strongest characters managed to break free. But it seemed possible that many would take any risk to escape, if only they had somewhere to go.

With the Governor of the Province, and the Roman Catholic Archbishop of Taegu, she talked things over; before very long, a home and vocational school was established. There were practically no funds to begin with, and local factory owners were astonished to see a 'foreign beggar' on their doorsteps, boldly and unashamedly pleading for furniture, bedding, old sewing and knitting machines, to help with this new venture.

There was some amusement, since 'foreigners' were assumed to be rich, but the self-possession and persuasive powers of the lively Western woman were irresistible. She seemed utterly convinced that these girls had to be helped and others accordingly fell in with her. Soon the home was sufficiently well equipped for occupation.

No difficulty arose in finding residents to fill the home, though the process of actually getting the girls there required ingenuity and perseverance. At first, Susie was forced to buy the girls out; later, as word spread, they found their own circuitous route to this new haven, and arrived on the doorstep, apprehensive but hopeful.

On opening-day rain was falling heavily and the girls who formed the first contingent were an unhappy-looking group, their make-up rain-spattered and their general appearance forlorn. Yet they slowly found themselves responding to this welcoming young woman who seemed perfectly prepared to treat them as human beings, and to respect their feminine status. They soon discovered that she and her staff, while of course having to keep certain aspects of the life of the home under control, loved them and trusted them.

In many ways Susie was one of them. With them she existed on the inadequate national diet, eating rice, pickled cabbage and thin vegetable soup. Like them, she slept on a mattress on the floor and took as little money for expenses as the lowest-paid worker in the home. Susie admits that the diet is not conducive to great physical stamina, but is convinced that sharing daily conditions is an important part of sharing the life of the people she finds herself among.

Working hours are from 5 a.m. until 11 at night for Susie; she aims at six hours' sleep, unless her rest is interrupted. There have been times when one of the girls, doubtful of her chance to rejoin society, is overwhelmed by all that she has undergone, and attempts suicide during the dark hours. Then, Susie is on the spot, to comfort and reassure, and point to a creative, hopeful attitude to the future. She is able to share her own reliance on the Christian faith for spiritual renewal; she can show that during periods of weariness and disappointment, experienced by everyone, herself included, it is God who gives the strength to continue.

As the news of the home spread, the brothel-owners were at first very active in their opposition. In one unpleasant scene, a girl was literally dragged from Susie's protection; this occurred when the train in which they were travelling had not yet left the station, and Susie left her charge for a moment to talk to a companion in an adjoining compartment. Gradually, opposition dwindled. After all, as Susie says plainly, if she took a thousand girls into her care, another thousand would soon be in the clutches of exploiters.

Not only human caring in a family setting, but also practical training is given to residents, to fit them for the new life they are encouraged to set out on. Trades such as dressmaking, hair-dressing and knitting with machines, are taught; slowly human dignity is restored. Successes have not numbered one hundred per cent, but results have proved very encouraging. The girls stay sometimes for one year, sometimes for as long as three years, or even more.

'Instruction in the Christian faith is not obligatory,' says Susie, 'but as the girls are looking for a way to wipe out the past and find a new hope, Christianity has a very strong appeal for them.' No doubt the invigorating example of Susie and her staff is a major influence on many of the girls. The easy and natural manner in which she talks of Our Lord as alive in every activity, suggests a confident, ever-growing faith that must attract many to its source.

Sometimes a resident's pitiful tale resolves in a real 'story-book' happy ending. One girl, daughter of a lowly island diving-woman, was tricked into a brothel. The girl, Miss A—, had suffered an unhappy home life and even when her father re-married, had not settled satisfactorily with her new step-mother. She seemed to be trapped in unhappiness. Then, through a relative, she heard of the home, managed to escape from her masters, and found refuge with Susie. Here, the repressed and cheerless personality flowered. Miss A— won all hearts by her friendly disposition and genuine desire to 'begin again'. She learned to knit, and to read (as she had avoided school), and was ultimately baptized as a Christian. At work on a farm, she met a young farm-worker and they fell in love. A proposal of marriage soon followed. Miss A— found the courage to speak of the dismal days of her past life. The young man urged her to put all this behind her and look to a joyful future, as his wife. Shortly afterwards, they were married. Such a story illustrates the dispelling of the girls' greatest fear, that they might be debarred from marriage and normal home-life.

Nowadays, a new departure for Susie is a project even more unusual, a concern likely to daunt social worker, teacher, dedicated Christian, all rolled into one. This is a farming venture, now three years old, which helps to support the girls' Home and also introduces scientific livestock farming among the peasants in the surrounding villages.

Childhood holidays in the country with one's grandmother are not a major instruction in farming expertise, but this did not deter the indefatigable Susie. It was plain to her educated and dispassionate eye that investment in farm projects and agricultural schools, along with the vocational training of boys and girls, were more effective, more lasting and more forward-looking, than spasmodic gifts of clothing and food. In her usual thorough and practical way, therefore, she began investigating possibilities.

In 1964 she was asked by the Archbishop of Taegu to take joint responsibility, with a local parish priest, Father Lee, for developing two hundred acres of uncultivated hillside, fifteen miles outside Taegu, and transforming it into a dairy farm. To farm cattle on the rough hillsides was an innovation, and to specialize in dairy-farming even rarer. The intention of the team was to raise a good high-yield herd, since although parts of Korea could be good for raising cattle, the local breeds are not milk-cows.

Goodwill was not enough to launch such a striking scheme. Agricultural and engineering experts were brought in, and plans were formed and implemented, and the exciting preliminary steps taken. Two heifers were sent from California, and many more imported ones bought on the spot. Besides the farm, an agricultural high-school, at the foot of the hill, was also envisaged, to teach improved farming methods.

The idea underlying this whole scheme was to bring hope for the future, producing good stock and helping to free the farmers from their seemingly inescapable poverty. It would also help to keep families together, and therefore go a long way towards keeping girls from prostitution. Moreover, there was plenty of employment given on immediate work to be carried out, whilst the project materialized. There were roads to be constructed, buildings to be erected, and the farm's own reservoir to be installed.

This imaginative scheme was bound to be costly. It was anticipated that the project might work out at no less than £90,000, an alarming prospect to anyone less enthusiastic and confident than Susie. The money had to be raised; undaunted, Susie embarked on a discipline of letter-writing and appeal by pen and word that is a story in itself. It is amazing that she was not stricken with writer's cramp. With the backing of various charitable bodies, including Oxfam, the money began to accrue. Naturally, her own church supported her vigorously. Susie was not – and is not – ashamed to ask for money for a cause that will mean to hundreds the difference between a living diet and near-starvation, between self-respect and hope-lessness.

The undeniable strength of the project, and Susie's un-flagging advocacy, have proved remarkably effective. There is still a tremendous lee-way to be made up financially and the appeal for funds is unremitting. But people and bodies from all walks of life, of varying churches and denominations, and no apparent religious beliefs at all, have been moved by the Younger story, and are making a practical response.

The boys' home has now been taken over by other suitable authorities; the girls' school must still be supported, and the hillside dairy farm and school maintained and developed. Susie's 'invitation year' to Korea has now lengthened into seven years, and she intends to remain in her adopted country for the rest of her life. She will not marry, because the love of Christ is *the* love of her life. Never for one moment does this attractive young woman give an impression of grim renunciation; rather, she seems to concentrate joyfully on the task in hand, whatever it happens to be, and so at present upon her large 'adopted family'.

Asked for an explanation, she puts it this way: 'Many people count the world well lost for love, and this can also apply to love of God.'

When Susie came back to England for a well-earned rest, she brought with her a letter to her parents from Taegu's Mayor, singing her praises in vivid tones. She might smile a little to hear herself described as an 'angel', but she values this tribute. For she finds her chosen way of life, though strenuous and demanding, completely fulfilling. Where Susie Younger is at work in Korea, west and east are successfully merged.

10

Designing the Church for To-day

LAURENCE KING

The nursery rhyme 'Oranges and Lemons', featuring the Great Bell of Bow, and a folk-tale of one Dick Whittington, thrice Lord Mayor of London, ensure a certain colourful posterity for an historic London church. St. Mary-le-Bow, Cheapside, is remarkable in many ways, particularly – from an architectural viewpoint – for Christopher Wren's tiered steeple, thrusting vigorously on the City's skyline.

Well-known too is the special involvement of the church with the people of London, and the legend which says that the true Cockney must be born within the sound of the world-famous Bow Bells. The romantic associations of more recent days cover a baptism of a grandchild of the Cockney 'Pearly King', and the patronage of Britain's Royal Family at the most contemporary restoration, including the sounding by Prince Philip of the first peal of Bow Bells, in 1961, after the restoration of the tower and steeple.

It is sombrely true that this church, like many others in the City's square mile, has undergone many vicissitudes through the centuries, suffering markedly during the Great Fire in 1666 and also in the holocaust of the Second World War. After the Great Fire it lay a gutted ruin and was re-built by Wren, when its tower and spire was thought by many to have been the Master's finest campanile. After the Second World War, little of the building survived the bombing, though the tower remained standing; the steeple was taken down, stone by stone, and stored until the tower had been suitably strengthened.

It was unthinkable that this church should not be restored, despite the obvious costliness of any such scheme. The Lord Mayor launched an appeal in 1956, and re-building began, under the direction of architect Laurence King. In his hands a two-fold operation commenced. The exterior of the church was to remain unchanged and the interior to be structurally the same; yet the whole building was to be re-designed to meet the special needs and purposes of the twentieth-century city church.

This is one of the dominating concerns of the life and work of Laurence King. Both in designing and building new churches and in restoring those of a former age, he forces us to acknowledge that the Church of God is a living organization; hence, any building to be erected that bears the title 'church', must cater for Christians of the twentieth century and reflect their requirements and activities.

He makes use, in conversation, of some quite startling images to express his firm conviction about the building or buildings in which the people of God meet together; the church as a building is to be a 'machine', or a 'shelter', or an 'instrument' for the 'ecclesia', the body of people meeting there who constitute the 'real' church, the living body of Christ. This viewpoint allows for a fine freedom of expression in ecclesiastical building and experiment can be as exciting and forward-looking as can be imagined. If we need today what can be summed up as a 'worshipping-space' and 'other meeting-space', this can be produced, in a variety of interesting ways, still with the accent on dignity and beauty, but with greater brightness and relevance to contemporary needs.

Laurence King is a man who stands confidently with one foot in the past and one in the present, an architect for whom the traditional and the modern blend without difficulty. History and archaeology hold great fascination for him. It is a natural step from this interest to that of a delight in restoring old churches, though he admits smilingly that 'not everyone is interested in preserving what is ancient!' He himself feels that the re-building of St. Mary-le-Bow is one of his most satisfying works, incorporating as it does the best of the past with the expression of the requirements of the present age.

A devoted churchman, he has been much influenced by contemporary interest in the re-structuring of public worship, known as the modern liturgical movement. Through this, and recognizing that the Church is one Common Family, he sees a drawing-together of the clergy and the laity. All are truly 'laity', since the word means 'people of God'; we are therefore all 'one body', one Christian fellowship, differentiated by church orders.

In past days, differences were stressed and this was made very manifest in ecclesiastical architecture, particularly in English church buildings, with their dividing chancel screen. Today's emphasis is upon freedom, openness and adaptability. St. Mary-le-Bow, which may well serve as a model for many of the churches of the future, now incorporates these features very strikingly. It is not now a matter, as formerly, of the Nave for the laity and the Chancel a 'holy of holies' for the clergy, with a division between. Under Laurence King's guidance, a low step constitutes the only division between priest and people. The Church's Table of the Eucharist stands free, just as much a Table of Christian Fellowship as an Altar.

There are no pews on the floor of the church, but chairs are set out as required; in this way, a very flexible method, larger congregations can easily be accommodated, but there need never be empty seats!

The blending of old and new in St. Mary-le-Bow is significant, and beautiful. This is not surprising; an awareness of things beautiful has characterized Laurence King since boyhood. This veneration for both beauty and age were felt keenly by him, even during his early years, and became a formative influence in his religious life.

He remembers how, as a small boy, he was taken by his father to look at old churches and other ancient buildings. Although his father was not by training an architect, he was a man deeply interested in the subject, and he took great pleasure in pointing out important features of the buildings to the lad at his side. In vivid phrase, he re-created the fascinating past and brought to life the ages that were gone, peopling the echoing passages and halls, and giving new and exciting meaning to both crumbling ruins and solid stone. There was no thought here of the past as 'dead'; it was merely something that led quite naturally to the present. Things then had been vital and relevant for their day, and remained full of delight even after the passing of time.

Church buildings in particular arrested the young Laurence King. In his mind, he began to recognize their differing architectural features, and to compare them. He began also to ask himself many questions. Sauntering through the quiet close, or entering the contrasting stillness of a city church, confronted by the flooding colours of the stained glass, or the compelling figure of the Christ on a rood-screen, he began to wonder about the inner meaning of the buildings. What were they really for? Why had they been put there in the first place? What actually went on there? Had it anything to do with the world outside? Back in the sunshine, these questionings in the boy's mind continued.

Thinking seemed to lead naturally to reading. He found himself flicking through the booklets and brochures that lay about on the tables in churches and church porches. They certainly told the story of the individual churches, but more than that, they also told the eager reader what lay behind the bricks and stones. Gradually, through the symbolism of the various architectural features, inner discernment began to dawn. This was what the church was all about! The past had led to the present, and beyond was the future. Buildings might in the days to come be different – why not – but the people of God whom they housed would inhabit the buildings as of old; generation after generation, in spite of the ebb and flow of the people's faith, would meet together to praise God and to be in companionship with one another. It was all-enduring.

This was the beginning of a spiritual journey. The pilgrim afterwards went on asking questions, and found many answers in the Established Church of this land, to which he became gradually more and more deeply attached.

Laurence chose architecture as his profession and his education in this sphere lay in the hands of the late Sir Albert Richardson. His talents flowered, and he became a tutor and lecturer at the Royal College of Art.

However, his future was not to be confined to academic circles alone. For one thing, a vast amount of travelling lay ahead. The major interruption to all careers, of the Second World War, took him to the Middle East and strengthened for him the fascination of the Christian architecture of the Holy Land and other parts of Asia Minor, on which he still lectures frequently. These lecture tours take him to all parts of the world, where his professional expertise and his churchmanship together produce an uniquely compelling speaker.

Nowadays, in his professional life, his work and his faith go together in a remarkable way. His practice is to a large extent concerned with church building, restoration and maintenance, bound up with his own personal interest in the reform of the liturgy and his life-long devotion to his church.

Travelling continues, but consists not only of organized lectures, but also of less formal journeys to quiet rural areas in this country. Here he talks to parochial church councils who are concerned about the restoration or re-building of their local churches. He is able to use his professional knowledge and considerable persuasive powers to explain contemporary views and to move conservative thinkers to a more adventurous outlook. His own enthusiasm must be infectious, to judge from the long list of parishes who are being caught up on the wave of new thought on church architecture, and who are looking to Laurence King to help them to express this through their church buildings. From the time, in the early thirties, when he worked on a church in his own Chelmsford diocese, until the present day, he has put his stamp upon parish churches all over the land. All bear the mark of this tall, elegant innovator.

Not only members of parochial church councils, but the public in general benefit from education in modern trends; people who confess to being non-church-goers can be the most reactionary of all when it comes to altering preconceived notions! One modern cathedral was castigated thus as 'not looking as a church should!' Laurence King shakes his head sadly at people for whom churches and the 'Gothic look' must be synonymous. He points out that the Gothic-type churches, built on the crest of a religious revival, endured because of their intrinsic strength, long after purely domestic buildings of the same age had vanished. People do not now expect houses to be necessarily built in period style, why therefore should churches?

As he further emphasizes, throughout the ages church buildings have undergone alterations, with pieces pulled down, added or redesigned, to suit the purposes of congregations, clergy or benefactors. The Church presents itself to the Glory of God in the way it deems best for the contemporary age, and this thesis continues to be worked out by Laurence King in small parish churches, in the houses of religious communities, and in cathedrals, such as Exeter, and Blackburn, where he is architect for the extension and completion of the cathedral.

Laurence King has no family of his own, but his interest in young people, and concern for tomorrow's generation, is intense. He holds definite opinions on the church buildings that will suit the future Christian community and these opinions have an ecumenical accent. Discussing the requirements of new housing estates, for example, he sees it as 'sheer madness' to erect various costly church buildings for different denominations. How much better, he suggests, to put up a common 'ecclesiastical shelter' that can be easily adapted to suit all denominations, that can be used by them at differing times, until church unity progresses even further. He seems to feel that the church of tomorrow will be forced to recognize the validity of such a viewpoint.

A pre-occupation with youth must of necessity engage much of Laurence King's working days, over and beyond church architecture. In a considerable portion of his practice, he is engaged on work in public schools and must be constantly aware of exciting new projects in the educational field. The greater stress on science, for instance, may demand suitable and adequate accommodation to be incorporated into traditional buildings.

It must be impossible for anyone involved in such activity, however great their love and reverence for the past, to be anything but mainly forward-looking. Impelled by the needs of tomorrow, Laurence King has placed his artistic gifts and professional training at the service of God and the community; through this, in school and in church, many young folk will surely discover a relevance and vitality in their surroundings that will enrich their experience of living, and give heightened significance to their religion. Schools need not be dull and drab; churches do not have to be dark and fusty; quite the reverse is not only feasible, but is actually being achieved.

As a practising member of the Anglican Church, Laurence King serves on the Southwark Diocesan Advisory Committee, and takes his place at Church Assembly. He is active in many church groups and his links with other religious traditions are strong. As might be expected, he is actively involved with the Anglican Council of Worship and the Arts.

Perhaps a good nut-shell view of the faith-and-work-relationship of Laurence King can be put as follows: 'Any good architect can obviously plan and carry through a church of sorts, but I think it is necessary to be a believer to bring a church scheme to life.' These are his words, and bringing such schemes to life is his profession, his Christian demonstration, and his delight.

TEN OF   TIME

TERM OF HIS TIME